Gender and Development

Women and Change in the Developing World

Series Editor
Mary H. Moran, Colgate University

Gender and Development

Rethinking Modernization and Dependency Theory

Catherine V. Scott

LYNNE
RIENNER
PUBLISHERS

BOULDER
LONDON

Published in the United States of America in 1995 by
Lynne Rienner Publishers, Inc.
1800 30th Street, Boulder, Colorado 80301

and in the United Kingdom by
Lynne Rienner Publishers, Inc.
3 Henrietta Street, Covent Garden, London WC2E 8LU

Library of Congress Cataloging-in-Publication Data
Scott, Catherine V. (Catherine Virginia)
   Gender and development : rethinking modernization and dependency
theory / by Catherine V. Scott.
   (Women and change in the developing world)
   Includes bibliographical references and index.
   ISBN 1-55587-410-X (alk. paper)
   1. Women in development. 2. Dependency. 3. Feminist theory.
   I. Title. II. Series.
HQ1240.S38 1995   94-22223
                                                              CIP

British Cataloguing in Publication Data
A Cataloguing in Publication record for this book
is available from the British Library.

Printed and bound in the United States of America

      The paper used in this publication meets the requirements
 ∞   of the American National Standard for Permanence of
      Paper for Printed Library Materials Z39.48-1984.

▲

Contents

▲ 1
Rereading Modernization and Dependency Theory

This study concerns itself with the way standard works in modernization and dependency theory have conceptualized, at a fundamental level, development, modernity, dependence, and revolution. Recent calls for moving beyond the stalemate that exists between the modernization (or developmentalist) and dependency paradigms through a blending of the best elements of each are premature, because each approach is deeply grounded in elaborate ideas that revolve around social constructions of gender differences. The recurring themes of modernity, development, self-reliance, and revolution are explored by many modernization and dependency theorists with a vision that is informed by gendered preoccupations and gendered conceptions about what it means to be modern and what it means to be self-reliant. If the two paradigms are "improved" upon or even discarded without examining the critical function that gender plays in elaborating modernization and dependency theory, the same types of dichotomies based on gender essentialisms are likely to recur. This study tries to give the implicit ideas about gender, tradition, and modernity a feminist critical reading so that future attempts to move beyond the two paradigms will be more self-conscious about and attentive to the extent to which we rely on gender to understand the meaning of development.

In addition to biases subject to well-known criticisms, modernization theory displays a deeper gendered structure. Object relations theory, an approach fruitfully employed by a number of feminist writers, helps to uncover the way in which challenges to modernization are framed. Dependency theory developed as a radical, often explicitly Marxist critique of orthodoxy in development studies, but it fails to challenge the social constructions of gender evident in the theory of its mainstream rival. These gendered assumptions are not only evident in theories of development and underdevelopment, but also are revealed in the dominant policies and practices of international

1

lending agencies such as the World Bank, and of revolutionary governments such as Angola and Mozambique, which seek alternative paths to development.

▲ The Stalemate in Development Theory

There seems to be a growing consensus that theorizing about political development in the Third World has reached an impasse and a period of introspection (Edwards 1989; Huntington 1987). It appears to many that debates between modernization (or developmentalist) and dependency frameworks have resulted in a stalemate and that a reconciliation of the two approaches is in order. In interesting language invoking a metaphor of battle, Smith (1985: 532) writes that this "clash of paradigms" has produced a crisis in Third World studies.

Suggestions for solving the crisis have included proposals for creatively combining modernization and dependency theory. In his analysis of the "Taiwan exception," Clark (1987: 328) suggests that "neither perspective is adequate by itself for explaining what has occurred in Taiwan," and "both provide some relevant and valuable insights." Others have tried to demonstrate that the two approaches are mirror images of the other or share basic similarities that would make a synthesis easy to accomplish. According to Vandergeest and Buttel (1988: 685),

> In modernization theory . . . evolution took place at the level of the nation-state; every country was following in the wake of the United States along a pre-determined series of stages. The neo-Marxist critique in its early dependency form . . . reassigned Third World countries to a new role in the grand evolutionary drama—it (sic) was now condemned to a pattern of peripheral or semiperipheral capitalist development.

Smith (1985: 556) argues that both developmentalism and dependency are "ideological"; the former justifies capitalism and the latter unites "Marxists and Third World nationalists in their mutual hatred of imperialism." He implies that dispensing with ideology could lead to the use of empirical and theoretical tools from both schools, "a cross-fertilization that brings the strengths of each into a new synthesis that leaves the old deadwood behind" (Smith 1985: 559).

Efforts to move beyond the purported orthodoxy of these two approaches have been particularly evident in African studies, where the language of crisis and catastrophe characterize much contemporary writing. A growing conviction that Africa has remained marginalized in the world capitalist economy and has failed to produce an East

Asian–style economic miracle has also produced calls for eclecticism and blending various approaches to political development in an effort to solve Africa's crisis. Shaw (1991: 193–194) has outlined a "mood of revisionism" that rejects both "orthodox modernization" and "orthodox materialism" and offers an invitation to theoretical pluralism concerning Africa's plight in the 1990s. He senses a new realism about the limits of modernization projects and revolutionary politics, and a new interest in the informal sector, popular participation, female production, and ecology, concerns that he believes the modernization and dependency paradigms have failed to address (Shaw 1991: 194). Nyang'oro (1989: 89) decries the stagnation affecting current scholarship and laments the continuing use of external actors as scapegoats for Africa's predicament. He calls for transcending the current state of confusion brought about by the inability of these two contending paradigms to provide understanding about the causes of African underdevelopment (Nyang'oro 1989: 100).

Similar criticisms of modernization and dependency theories are often invoked by those who lobby for a new synthesis and a transcendence of the prevailing paradigms—although the transcendence actually entails borrowing the theoretical and empirical "tools" of both. Methodologically, modernization theory has been shown to make arbitrary and artificial distinctions between traditional and modern societies. Such formalism reduced the history of Third World societies to ideal types or models that proved "too stifling, too tyrannical, and ultimately too sterile for the empirical work they sought to organize" (Smith 1985: 536). In their review of the seven-volume series, "Studies in Political Development," produced over a decade by the Social Science Research Council (SSRC) Committee on Comparative Politics, Holt and Turner (1975: 987) describe the committee's efforts as "intuitive empirical generalization" because of the relative lack of "rigorous concept formation, systematic analysis, or the development of interrelated propositions." Another frequent criticism is the ethnocentric positioning of the West as the universal model of development for Third World countries (Randall and Theobald 1985: ch. 2). Dependency theory has also been criticized on methodological grounds. Numerous writers have complained that dependence has been vaguely or tautologically defined and cannot be measured effectively (Ruccio and Simon 1989: 134). It has also been faulted for an inadequate exploration of the role of the state, varieties of dependence, class relations, and culture (Vandergeest and Buttel 1988: 685).

Both sets of criticisms assume that methodological mistakes and ahistorical analyses can be rectified and that aspects of each paradigm can be used to create a newer and better means of understanding and managing development in the Third World. In so doing, those who call for a synthesis ignore the continuing power of the West over the Third World and the way in which much scholarship within these two paradigms continues to produce particular meanings about development, modernization, dependence, and revolution (Mohanty 1991b: 54–55). Said (1979) has described the way in which Western theory about the Orient has served as a discourse of domination and authority, and de Groot (1991: 108) has highlighted the relevance of examining historical and cultural influences that have shaped contemporary discussions of development. She traces the continuity between nineteenth-century European encounters with Third World societies and more recent characterizations of development by exploring the dichotomous juxtapositions that were used to contrast European and non-European societies, and the extent to which presentations of non-Western women as backward and oppressed victims played a pivotal role in the depictions of "backward" societies generally (de Groot 1991: 111). Johnston's (1991) analysis of the disciplinary power of modernization theory in identifying anomalies that impede development, establishing hierarchies of traditional/modern, and setting up the means for reforming or rehabilitating recalcitrant traditional polities also demonstrates the importance of analyzing the way in which development theory creates its subject. In Johnston's (1991: 164) words: "Modernization theory cannot hope to rid itself of the traditional because its very existence depends upon the logical opposition between traditional and modern."

Such critical works demonstrate the importance of exploring the way in which prevailing cultural and political images, conceptions, language, and historical legacies have shaped and continue to influence discourse about development and modernization in the Third World. They attempt to go beyond debates within paradigms to ask more fundamental questions about the way in which key questions are framed, how problems are delineated, and what kinds of solutions to the problems are offered. More critical analyses, in other words, have been concerned with the way in which theory itself has been produced and creates hegemonic consensus, in this case about the meaning of modernization, development, and revolution. Modernization and dependency theory are hegemonic in that many fundamental questions, particularly about the gendered meaning of development, require no elaboration; they constitute the "common sense" about political development and dependence in the Third World.[1] Samuel Huntington (1987: 3) has complained about such vigorous critique. In his view such explorations have meant that "the theory displaced the thing as the primary focus of inquiry" in development studies. This study seeks to move beyond both the theory and the thing in an effort to ask critical questions about the production of themes about modernity, development, and dependence from a masculine standpoint.

▲ Modernity and the Masculine Standpoint

This study is interested in delineating how contemporary Western theorizing—mainly in the United States—about modernity and development is anchored firmly in pervasive social constructions of gender differences. Modernity has been envisioned, particularly by modernization theorists, in opposition to a feminized and traditional household, and the achievement of modernity has been portrayed by many modernization theorists as a power struggle with the feminine on the way to "maturity." For dependency theorists, the achievement of autonomy and self-reliance conveys a definition of revolutionary development that conceptualizes it as a set of masculine challenges, to be overcome, through separation from and then modernization of the female-headed household. Self-reliance entails the application of science and technology to the inert forces of nature and increasing control over those forces that cause stagnation and underdevelopment.

For modernization theory, development requires the emergence of rational and industrial man, an individual who is receptive to new ideas, acknowledges different opinions, is punctual and optimistic, and believes that rewards should be distributed on the basis of universalistic rules. This change entails a move to the city, away from the powerful pull of village, farm, and "tribe." The counterpart to modern man is the modern and efficient state, one that evolves toward an increasingly differentiated capacity to penetrate society and evolves new means of solving the problems of development. The state achieves new mechanisms of domination and power, an "ability to get what [it] wants from people over whom [it] seeks to exercise power" (LaPalombara 1971: 209). For dependency theory, rationalized revolutionary politics by a subordinated class of men promises to break the hold of stagnant tradition and usher in self-reliant, self-creating, and autonomous development.

Although I intend to argue that both theoretical approaches are grounded in somewhat similar masculinist notions of what it means to be modern, I disagree that the two approaches are essentially similar, possess similar flaws, and can be synthesized to achieve a fuller understanding of the development problematique. Modernization theory is grounded in a particular tradition of liberalism that calls for very limited state intervention and assumes the primacy of the market. This brand of liberalism has also produced a view of women

as closer to nature, justified a sexual division of labor between men-
tal (male) and physical (female) labor, and embraced a formal
rather than substantive conception of equality (Jagger 1983: 46–47).
Given its liberal grounding, I will argue that liberal modernization
theory cannot constitute an adequate foundation for sustainable
well-being for men and women in the Third World.

Dependency theory, following Marx, has a materialist grounding
that focuses on the systemic and structural characteristics of life and
has more promise than modernization theory. In its efforts to examine humans in their "actual historical situation," dependency theory
offers a more accurate view of women's lives, "the kind of labor they
perform, the ways in which this labor is organized, and the social relations that women form with each other and with men as a result of
their labor and its mode of organization" (Jagger 1983: 63). Dependency theory, however, taking its cue from Marx, also tends to view
women's labor as natural and bound to the household, while the
public realm is a privileged location for revolutionary activity. I will
argue that dependency theory and revolutionary practice offer a better but still partial foundation for sustainable well-being for both
men and women in the Third World.

▲ Meanings of Masculinity and Definitions of
Modernization and Development

The definitions, conceptions, and language used to define and describe political development are interwoven with masculine meanings and have the imprimatur of masculine preoccupations. A number of feminist-inspired criticisms of Western political thought have
attempted to trace the operation and influence of masculine concerns, and I draw on some of this work in my efforts to subject modernization and dependency theory to feminist criticism and analysis.

Brown (1988) and Di Stefano (1991a) have illuminated the influence of masculinity in the work of Aristotle, Hobbes, Marx, Mill,
and Weber. Brown (1988: 4) argues that the "historical relationship
between constructions of manhood and constructions of politics
emerges through and is traced upon formulations of political foundations, political order, citizenship, action, rationality, freedom, and
justice." While tracing a line of continuity in the relationship between manhood and politics, Brown also demonstrates the uneven
character of the relationship. For example, while for the Greeks "a
real man is independent of the realm of necessity, of constraints by
others, and of needs and desires of his own body," Machiavellian
manhood is concerned with controlling the unknown, represented

by women, and with achieving self-mastery (Brown 1988: 55, 88–90). Di Stefano (1991a: 58) characterizes masculinity as a "bundle of beliefs, attitudes, and goals that have some coherence and characteristic structure," and finds distinct versions of masculinity—heroic, productive, and disciplinary, respectively—in the thought of Hobbes, Marx, and Mill. Thus she also suggests that the ethos and configurations of manhood and masculinity vary but have continuity and an identifiable structure and content.

This analysis of modernization and dependency theory makes a similar claim. In an effort to illuminate both the continuity and variation in the persistent masculine emphases of these two approaches, I rely on three critical approaches that help to lay bare the common themes of masculinity and development: public/private and related dichotomies, object relations theory, and metaphorical language that characterizes development as a battle, struggle, or war.

▲ Public/Private, Modern/Traditional

A number of writers have traced the connections between nature, women, and the private sphere in Western political thought. Ortner (1974: 73) based her arguments concerning the "universal fact of women's subordination" on the claim that every society views women as closer to, or a part of, nature, and therefore it is "natural" to subordinate women (Ortner 1974: 69). Ortner's claims have been challenged by those who argue that the concepts of nature and culture themselves have multiple meanings that have varied over time (Bloch and Bloch 1980). Nevertheless, there is an important tradition in Western political thought that has linked women and nature in opposition to culture and men. Lloyd's (1984: 2) discussion of the "maleness" of reason locates the Greek connection between women and nature in women's capacity to conceive. In sexual reproduction, the "clear determination of males" was contrasted with the passivity of the mother, who "only" provided the matter that received the determination (Lloyd 1984: 3).

While the ancient tradition was overt in its alignment of males with reason and females with intuition, later philosophers produced "variations on the theme" (Rooney 1991: 82). Rousseau, for example, proposed a complementarity between male/reason and female/nature. The private domain was conceived as a haven of "virtue and tenderness" from the corruption of public life (Lloyd 1984: 78). Locke's break with traditional authority through arguments about the benefits of contracts and the rationalization of public life led to a firmer split between gendered conceptions of public and private, with the latter associated with women, "sense impression, and desires" (Elshtain 1981: 119). As Charlton (1989: 25) notes, liberalism based its claims on controlling state power, while the "private sphere continued as the non-political domain of individual and family."

Given the diversity of meanings given to the public/private distinction in Western thought, it is important to specify the links made between the two by modernization and dependency theorists. For modernization theorists, the public realm is a space populated by men who have left the private realm of village and "tribe" to become modern. In a pervasive contrast, the family, household, and village are treated as obstacles to the achievement of modernity. The public realm of authority is where the state achieves greater "capacity, equality, and differentiation" (Coleman 1971: 74–75) and transcends the world of diffuse and undifferentiated tradition. Modernity results in a new capacity to "plan, implement and manipulate new change" and in the enhancement of rationality (Coleman 1971: 78–80).

Modernization is also viewed as synonymous with urbanization and is frequently contrasted with the stagnation of rural life. Huntington (1968: 72) describes the city as the "locus of new economic activities, new social classes, new culture and education," while the rural areas are described as "tradition-bound" and in fact so radically different from the city that they constitute a separate nation. Binder (1971: 35–36) states that a "distinctively urban way of life" is associated with the development process. For modernization theorists, the creation of viable bureaucracies and states with the capacity to penetrate the rural areas and establish an *"effective presence"* throughout a territory requires the rationality, efficiency, and dynamism that they associate with city life. A key challenge for the leadership of developing countries is to bring modernity to the rural areas, "regardless of what may be the views . . . of those who are the objects of government policy" (LaPalombara 1971: 209). This description of urban modernity and the urban-rural gap reformulate the public and private dichotomies that pit reason against nature, lightness against darkness, culture against nature, and man against woman.[2]

In fact, themes of struggle are pervasive in modernization theory and are often couched in evolutionary terms and metaphors that contrast the developing polity with their mature counterparts, depict movement from one to the other as something that entails struggle, and equate development with domination. Verba (1971: 292) writes that capacity may be *"the* underlying dimension of development," because it refers to the "growth in the capacity of governmental institutions to make and enforce decisions." Huntington's (1968:1) concern with order leads him to define development in the terms of Hobbes's Leviathan: "The most important political distinction among countries concerns not their form of government but their degree of government."

Perhaps most important, modernization is achieved through the market, as distinct from the private and "non-economic" sphere of the home (Jagger 1983: 144). Markets allow the talents of acquisitive, entrepreneurial, and competitive men to flourish, and creates bonds among men that preclude ties to family, village, household, and "tribe." The state's role is a minimalist one. As it develops the requisite functional specialization and differentiation, it becomes more capable of managing conflicts that might arise between men. The state also provides the framework for the realization of entrepreneurial talents. In keeping with liberal precepts, society is conceived of as being "theoretically outside of state control, . . . a realm of non-state economic activities resting on the institution of private property," (Charlton 1989: 25) and in modernization theory's formula, composed of rational economic men who will accomplish the necessary economic breakthrough for capitalist-style development.

The corpus of liberal modernization theory says almost nothing explicit about women, yet at the same time—as I will show—it rests upon very gendered foundations. Associations between tradition and powerful, socially constructed traits of women play a crucial role in elaborating modernization theory and in outlining the contours of the modern polity. Crucial meanings about the process of modernization, obstacles to it, and celebrations of the modern are laden with gender categories, associations, and attributes.

Dependency theorists would no doubt, following Marx's lead, reject the liberal distinction between public and private as an ideological device that obscures the basis of workers' and women's oppression. Following Marx and Engels, dependency theorists would view the family as a social relationship that reflects the mode of production. Just as capitalism was viewed by Marx and Engels as particularly exploitative of women, dependency theorists would view the colonial and capitalist mode of production as exploitative of women as well. Nevertheless, dependency theorists share a tendency with Marxists to view sexual and family relations as part of the private sphere and to consider the private less central than the public realm (Jagger 1983: 146). Thus male dominance tends to be viewed as a secondary contradiction that can be addressed only through the transformation of the social relations of production.

Class relations and subordinate relations between center and periphery in the world capitalist economy thus take precedence in dependency theory; other locations of struggle, contradiction, and conflict are given less attention. Class struggle in the public realm promises to usher in a revolutionary polity that, interestingly, is heavily

industrialized and characterized by scientific and technological innovation. Dependency theory's definition of self-reliance is the rationally administered polity that has escaped the stagnation of dependence through revolution.

While classic texts on dependency theory fail to include explicitly an analysis of the "woman question," its definitions of exploitation, self-reliance, revolution, and development also have gendered
associations. As with modernization theory, the framework of pub-
lic/private and modern/traditional provides a lens for viewing the
gendered discourse of dependency theory.

▲ Object Relations Theory

The emergence of the Enlightenment emphasis on progress, science,
and the transformation of agrarian life coincided with structural
changes in the family in the West during the industrial revolution.
Object relations theory has been fruitfully used to describe the way
in which a gendered sense of self has developed in middle-class, nuclear families in the West. It has been used to trace how this gendered sense of self has framed, for example, ideas about political
obligation and portrayals of human nature (Hirschmann 1989; Di
Stefano 1991a).

Object relations theory is an account of human development
that emphasizes the role of early infantile experience in creating a
"core identity" in which gender is a central element (Flax 1983: 251).
"Psychological birth" for boys entails separation and individuation
from the chief caretaker—in many bourgeois families in the West,
the mother—who is perceived as omnipotent (Chodorow 1989: 34).
The process of individuation is more conflictual for boys because
"both mother and son experience the other as the definitive 'other'"
(Hartsock 1983: 238). Girls, on the other hand, experience less conflictual and contradictory desires for fusion and independence because girls see themselves as similar to the caretaker. Boys come to
define masculinity as that which does not involve women: denigration and devaluation of the feminine serve the boy's need to achieve
autonomy and separation from the mother (Chodorow 1989: 51).
The challenge in male psychic development is achieving independence, which "produces a conception of agency that abstracts individual will . . . out of the context of the social relationships within
which it develops and within which it is exercised, because it sees
those relationships as threatening by definition" (Hirschmann 1989:
1231). Psychological development and cultural prescriptions work to
"define masculinity in contrast to maternally defined femininity" (Di

Stefano 1991a: 45). Males must identify with an abstract cultural stereotype; masculinity is idealized, and the masculine sense of self as separate, distinct, and "even disconnected" develops against the feminine (Hartsock 1983: 239).

Yet separation and individuation are usually only partial achievements because of the ambivalence that accompanies the symbiosis between mother and child (Flax 1983: 252–253). There is ambivalence surrounding the conflicting desires for fusion and independence that is rarely fully resolved: "instead, it simmers restlessly in the unconscious, an easy target of reevocation in adult life" (Di Stefano 1991a: 39). Identification with the father and with culturally defined masculinity helps to overcome the ambivalent relationship and helps to maintain gender differences. It also helps create an "intricate admixture of metaphysics, cognitive style, and sexual metaphor" (Keller 1990: 45), a distinctive view of the world of politics.

Object relations theory can help illuminate the way in which development challenges have been framed and explored, especially by modernization theorists. The theory is less concerned with the psychological needs of individuals. It is not an essentialist statement about "men's upbringing" or categorical statements about "the way men think." Object relations is useful for exploring certain concerns that resonate in theories of political development and in psychological accounts of human development and the development of a core gender identity. It provides an account of achieved masculinity that helps us understand a number of otherwise puzzling preoccupations that recur in the modernization and dependency literature, especially the former.

One particularly interesting theme of modernization theory is a depiction of the rural village and "tradition" as something that must be struggled against. The struggle is often presented in strikingly psychological terms and depicts an ambivalence toward the comforts of tradition and the security it provides. Rostow (1960: 26), for example, locates one source of nationalism in the the traditional society's failure to protect men *(sic)* from humiliation by foreigners. Rostow (1960: 30) also describes the modernization process—from "take-off" to the "drive to maturity"— as one that takes place in two stages. First there is a group that is still "weighted too heavily with interests and attitudes from the traditional past." The second stage produces "a generation of men who were not merely anxious to assert national independence but were prepared to create an urban-based modern society." It is significant that Rostow frames the requisites for take-off in language that resonates with object relations accounts of masculine reactions against "tradition," the realm of clan, family, and household. Object relations helps explain the emphasis on the necessity of breaking ties with tradition in order to achieve modernity and the difficulties that accompany efforts to overcome those traditional attachments.

Similar concerns are evident in Pye's (1971b: 131) analysis of the identity and legitimacy crises faced by leaders in the Third World. He calls on dynamic leadership to resolve "identity problems" and create the "basis for national unity." Pye cites the need for individualistic leadership to overcome the problems of a parochial elite culture, one that "vacillates between the extremes of aggressively seeking modernization and of articulating parochial sentiments." Resolving the identity crisis thus means separation from and transcendence of traditional society, which threatens the unity of national identity.

The themes of struggle, separation, and ambivalence about "modern man's" relationship to tradition plays a different role in dependency theory, but some of the dilemmas and concerns suggested by object relations theory are evident in characterizations of underdeveloped societies and the goals of self-reliance and autonomy. For Walter Rodney (1981: 3), genuine independence means that a nation, like a child, no longer relies on others and can achieve self-sustaining growth. Samir Amin (1974b: 393) emphasizes the importance of autonomy and self-reliance in order to achieve "development in the true sense." For dependency theorists, the worldwide spread of capitalism has subsumed various precapitalist modes of production and rendered them incapable of reproducing themselves. In the theory, revolutionary leaders of dependent societies are not locked in struggle with the forces of "tradition," because "tradition" has been effectively and violently undermined. Dependence upon world capitalism must be broken through liberation struggles and revolution. However, like the ambivalent relationship between colonizer and colonized, the discourse of dependency theory places benign faith in the model of growth and development in the West. As Shivji (1976: 27–28) puts it,

> The African people cannot liberate themselves from their technological backwardness without the modern methods of natural science, nor can they liberate themselves from their oppressive social organization without scientific, social methods.

In this framework, "traditional" or "precapitalist" societies are rendered exploited victims of world capitalism. The precapitalist/private/household is the site of superexploitation and the location of the "backward" social practices. Liberation politics seeks to transcend underdevelopment and "create a rational and humane society and achieve the domination of the present over the future (and past), bringing the historical process under control" (Shapiro 1976: 148).

Thus, from the perspective of object relations theory, feminized tradition is the site of struggle and resistance—and a point of reference for modernization theorists who are eager to promote the emergence of individual leaders capable of solving the crises of national unity in "developing" societies. For dependency theorists, world capitalism has reduced underdeveloped countries to a state of childlike dependence: revolution promises to usher in autonomous, self-reliant development.

▲ Heroic Leadership and Development as Domination

Although traditional societies were rarely described in any detail by modernization theory, powerful meanings were attached to the idea of "traditional society" and tradition was often portrayed as something to be overcome or struggled against. The achievement of modernity required heroic leadership that could succeed in the tasks of domination and battle over the dangerous forces of tradition. In "soft state" theory, the contemporary incarnation of modernization theory (discussed below), heroic leadership plays a critical role in bringing about modernity. Heroic and solitary leadership is also a subsidiary yet important theme in modernization theory of the 1960s. McClelland (1976: 303) explains that "economic development has proceeded most rapidly in countries where the entrepreneurial spirit has met the least resistance from traditionalism." The Social Science Research Council portrays solitary leadership arrayed against a traditionalism that threatens with disorder and chaos as a major challenge faced by the developing polity. Integration (national unity) and penetration (establishing an effective presence) are presented as necessary to regulate the tensions and conflicts inevitably encountered in the transition to modernity (Coleman 1971: 740).

While dependency theory does not focus on the power of traditional society—rather, it has been subsumed and destroyed by capitalism—it does frame revolutionary politics in heroic terms. Revolutions require enlightened leadership versed in the modern sciences, knowledgeable about the latest techniques in order to transform the material base of society. The hierarchy of domination ascribed to center-periphery relations and "the whole chain of constellations of metropole and satellites" (Frank 1966: 19) needs to be challenged by a "new generation of scientists from the underdeveloped countries" (Frank 1966: 31). Dependency theory makes a link between the importance of scientific (modern) knowledge and the ability to "apply" it to Third World societies that is both individualistic and elitist. Development is often presented as a series of choices that allow men to apply successfully the correct scientific techniques to the problem of dependence (Amin 1974b: 28). Dependency theory also contains an image of an enlightened and heroic male leadership that challenges dependency through public revolutionary politics. Thus, while the emphasis on heroic and solitary leadership struggling against the forces of tradition that threaten to set back the clock on development is more pervasive in modernization theory, dependency theory contains its own version—scientifically minded men ushering in a new era of continuous development and independence.

▲ "Soft State": Updated Modernization Theory for Africa

Goran Hyden is another theorist who has argued that the modernization and dependency paradigms have been exhausted and that development theory in Africa requires new thinking based on an appreciation of the "historical specificity" and uniqueness of Africa's place in world history:

> What can be done to help Africa out of the present crisis? It is clear that the answer is not "more of the same." Neither more funds, nor better planning and more management development . . . will make a difference. Everybody must accept that there is no ready-made answer. What lies ahead is a painful search for alternatives (1983a: xii).

Rejecting both the 1960s focus on domestic politics and the 1970s proposals for disengagement from the world economy, Hyden (1987: 119) applauds the return of theorizing to an analysis of "hidden" social processes and informal social structures.

Perhaps more than any other contemporary theorist, Hyden has been a key contributor to the view that "there is a problem with the African state" (Doornbos 1990: 179). Hyden argues that the state lacks structural roots in African societies: it is "suspended in mid-air" and is "soft" (Hyden 1983a: 195) because producers are firmly ensconced in a peasant mode of production, defined as a "situation where the bulk of rural producers possess their own land, use very simple technologies, and are only marginally incorporated into the market economy" (Hyden 1983a: 71). The "economy of affection" is the cultural reflection of these material conditions, defining the "underlying moral or cultural imperatives" that govern peasant communities (Lemarchand 1989: 34). The economy of affection constitutes a network of kin-group ties that serves as a basis for social maintenance, informal economic activity, and basic survival (Hyden 1983a: 11–15). The strength of the economy of affection leads Hyden to characterize African countries as "societies without states" (Hyden 1983a: 7). He has developed these related ideas in a series of books and articles, beginning with the publication of *Beyond Ujamaa in Tanzania: Underdevelopment and an Uncaptured Peasantry* (1980). The most significant change in his overall argument occurred in 1983, with the publication of *No Shortcuts to Progress: African Development Management in Perspective*. In what Kasfir (1986: 338) describes as a "breathtaking change of heart," Hyden embraced the market and argued that capitalist development was the only viable strategy available for transforming the economy of affection and halting the peasants' ability to escape state power.

This framing of the challenges to development has a very familiar ring to it. The chief obstacle to development is the economy of affection (or "tradition"), those "embedded informal mechanisms which stand in the way of a viable state" (Lemarchand 1989: 37). The economy of affection is guided by the reciprocities and moral imperatives (or, "clan, village, and 'tribe'"), while the state is governed by more rational and less parochial principles. Finally, tradition must be challenged through the discipline of the market, and the slumbering entrepreneurial spirit, stifled by the soft state, should be awakened.

Mamdani (1985) and Hyden and Peters (1991) have noted that soft-state theory is recycled and updated modernization theory which, as Mamdani (1985: 190) aptly notes, has been replaced with a new terminology "to suit the changed ideological context of the 1980s." Hyden and Peters (1991: 326) argue that Hyden's paradigm reproduces the "the nineteenth-century dichotomy of two different societies," one precapitalist (traditional) and based in affective relations, and the other a capitalist (modern) society based on instrumental and impersonal relationships. But, like other critics of Hyden (e.g., Cliffe 1987; Kasfir 1986; Lemarchand 1989), Mamdani and Peters are more concerned with the empirical validity and historical accuracy of Hyden's claims. My argument in Chapter 3 is that Hyden resurrects, in powerful and provocative ways, the same kinds of gendered social constructions that played a key role in the production and influence of modernization theory. While the empirical validity and historical accuracy of Hyden's claims certainly deserve further scrutiny, this reexamination should be accompanied by a feminist interrogation of his work that tries to trace the way in which gender marks his arguments at a more fundamental level. This need is especially urgent with soft state theory because it has spawned a whole body of related literature that makes the approach one of the most powerful in contemporary theorizing about African politics.

Some of the most noteworthy aspects of Hyden's writings are the rich metaphorical, symbolic, and fundamentally masculinist devices he uses to contrast precapitalist and capitalist relations. For example, with the provocative description of the economy of affection as an "economy other than a market economy" (Hyden 1980: 19), the reader is invited to imagine a space where nurturance, reciprocity, and familial relations govern social life. The development project is then defined as one that will "remove the remnants" of the economy of affection (Hyden 1983a: 212). Who can cut the bonds that connect "man" to the economy of affection? The rational economic entrepreneur of modernization theory resurfaces as a "bourgeois class" capable of transcending the tenacious networks of reciprocity and kinship that threaten state power. Hyden also expresses alarm about the economy of affection taking over the state. As Hyden and Peters (1991: 324) explain, the economy of affection is viewed as a kind of virus spreading into both market and state and, in the language of object relations theory, threatening engulfment. I argue in Chapter 3 that we should take Hyden's metaphors and the symbolic content of his language seriously because it helps explicate the continuity of themes in both modernization and soft-state theory. Furthermore, Hyden's language, I argue, is more than just a stylistic quirk. Metaphorical language uses gender subtly to establish the superiority of capitalist modernity to precapitalist tradition. The repeated metaphorical gendered pairings produce a powerful definition of modernity that is purportedly "value-free" but which consistently treats precapitalist/tradition as inferior, incomplete, and even dangerous.

Hyden also provides a gendered dichotomy of public and private that anchors his arguments about the benefits of the market and the damaging consequences of an economy of affection that maintains the upper hand in the standoff between state and society. For example, he faults the economy of affection for producing parochial attitudes, and praises urban life for enforcing "punctuality, calculability, and exactness" (Hyden 1986: 61). Hyden powerfully juxtaposes the logic of the economy of affection with the logic of the modern state. While the former is partial, fragmented, and buried in "hidden" processes, the latter is the universal, integrationist, and rational.

In one of his most recent formulations, Hyden (1992: 11) replaces the categories of traditional and modern with "god-given" and "man-made" in reference to two types of political structures. The former represent the ties of family and community; the latter represent the civic structures erected to "regulate political behavior and interactions." Man-made structures are "necessary to transcend the limitations of community" and represent an "inevitable progress toward greater civility and equality in interpersonal and intergroup relations"

(Hyden 1992: 11, 20–21). A second (and, in my view, less significant) change in Hyden's thinking is evident in some of this recent writing. He seems to appreciate the vibrance of the "primordial" realm and proposes an intermediate role for it in the transition to the development of more civic societies. He allows, for example, that perhaps the state should "provide more space to the economy of affection" in order to "improve public management" (1990: 263). A certain sharing of responsibilities between government and informal organizations might be necessary during the transition to a "hardened" state.

Finally, Hyden relies on powerful images and metaphors of battle and war to express the challenges and obstacles to modernity and the rewards that accompany capitalist modernization. One key challenge is "penetration," a militaristic and sexually charged term that promises to bring about triumph over the economy of affection. "Breaking the backbone" of the economy of affection and "cutting the bonds" that have allowed it to dangerously "infiltrate" the state are presented as important tasks for African leaders (Hyden 1986: 70; Hyden 1983a: 91). In order to accomplish the task, "men of destiny" must emerge who can "throw off the bonds imposed by the economy of affection" (Hyden 1983a: 24). The achievement of modernity is a feat of historic proportions because it signifies successful struggle over insinuating and threatening tradition. Modernity requires heroic action on the part of men.

It is perhaps no coincidence that Hyden's changing view on the role of the economy of affection coincided with a change in focus by the World Bank, one of the leading lending agencies in Africa. In the second part of this book I look at the relationship between theory and practice: modernization and structural adjustment, and dependency theory and revolution.

▲ From Theory to Practice: Structural Adjustment or Revolution?

After a decade of seeking to make women visible through activities such as the United Nations Decade for Women, the creation of women's departments in national governments, and the grassroots political activity of countless women's groups, the World Bank went from barely mentioning women in a 1981 report to repeated references to women's issues in a crucial report issued in 1989. Like Hyden, the Bank claims that "responsibility for Africa's economic crisis is shared" (World Bank 1989: 2). It also consistently claims, however, that "poor public resource management and bad policies" rather than declining terms of trade or other international factors are the major sources of Africa's economic decline (World Bank 1989: 23). In order to create an "enabling environment" for growth

> future development strategies should favor women. Government and donors should help women's groups to contribute more fully to economic and social development through training and access to credit by giving them equal status in their dealings with formal institutions (World Bank 1989: 60).

This recommendation conflicts with the Bank's simultaneous call for a minimalist and neutral state, one that merely enforces contracts and creates a framework for transactions between individuals who are not encumbered by household duties. The Bank's focus on entrepreneurs also ensures that future development policies under its aegis will not favor women, because the vision of development embraced by the Bank is one that accepts the public/private distinction of liberal modernization theory. Women's roles within the household are conceived of as "natural," even though the Bank suggests the implementation of a host of timesaving devices to relax "some of the constraints on women in their household nurturing capacity" (World Bank 1989: 87).

This vision of women in development is ultimately not "woman-friendly" (Jones 1990). The Bank in effect takes Hyden's suggestion about an intermediate role for the "economy of affection" and assigns it the role of "safety net" during the painful transformation to a more efficiently run capitalist economy. Women continue to be defined in terms of procreative, childrearing, and "household economy" functions, but they are also made the new "targets" of government policies and the recipients of greater bureaucratic discipline and control. Although the bulk of Chapter 4 is devoted to an analysis of the the Bank's worldview, I also examine the formulation of the woman question within the Southern African Development Coordination Conference (SADCC). SADCC's acceptance of the integrationist framework, while ignoring the effect of the masculinist role of the state in its liberal, capitalist, and bureaucratic capacities, demonstrates the continuing power of modernization theory and practice and reflects the increasing hegemony of World Bank and related discourse on women in Africa.

Marxism and dependency theory share with liberalism and modernization theory a tendency to posit public production as a key activity that encourages the development of individuals who are "rational, active, many sided, scientifically minded, and in general capable of understanding and promoting a progressive view" (Thompson

1986: 109). I argue in Chapter 6 that revolutionary governments in Southern Africa have focused on the primacy of public production ("winning the battle of production") and have defined the politics of the household as a secondary contradiction. According to the leadership, women must participate in the modernity project through revolutionary public activity. The postrevolutionary period promises to usher in material growth, which in turn will transform gender relations.

Dependency theory's emphasis on class conflict finds its counterpart in the revolutionary's exhortation to women to engage in public production in order to escape from ignorance and backwardness. In this sense, the binary opposition of tradition/backward and modern/progressive is embraced by revolutionary discourse. The lack of any sustained analysis of the dynamics and contradictions of household politics and gender relations has made revolutionary governments vulnerable to opposition movement claims that the counterrevolutionary movement represents a return to the "essence" of traditional gender roles that ultimately seek to buttress male power. Thus the real accomplishments of the revolution are threatened by reactionary support of women's "proper" role in society. While the dynamics of revolution and counterrevolution certainly obey other factors, such as the regional dominance of South Africa, ethnic conflict, and so forth, discursive struggles over gender relations need to be examined as well.

▲ Methodology

This book is not really about women in development. The Women in Development (WID) literature is vast and has been important in, for example, challenging "both the definition of work and the method of data collection" in development studies (Tinker 1990: 46). WID theorists and practitioners have also attempted to adapt development theory to take class into account, reevaluate women's work, and assess the impact of debt and structural adjustment on women. On the other hand, more recent feminist scholarship has challenged the very meaning of development and has proposed new visions that attempt to go beyond the liberal and Marxist-inspired visions (e.g., Sen and Grown 1987; Shiva 1988).

In addition, except for a few passing references, I am not so interested in uncovering and documenting the explicitly sexist treatment of the role of women by modernization and dependency theorists. While some of the references do indicate a sexist view of women (and the vast silences are perhaps even more important) the concern of this book is not with establishing the misogynist or sexist attitudes of these theorists, which, however, is also important, and continues to be carried out by WID theorists and practitioners. Finally, this book is not about "making women visible." In fact, I believe that women are very much present in the literature on modernization and dependency theory. The space they occupy, though often in the shadows, provides an important opposition upon which ideas about development are constructed.

My method is what Di Stefano (1991a: 10) has called rereading— "the process of reassessing texts (canonical as well as minor works) in the light of new questions and deliberately specified, often politicized, perspectives." Two claims guide this methodology. The first is that feminist interrogation can pose interesting questions that the texts have not posed directly to themselves. For example, how is political development defined? What aspects of human nature are assumed to be the most salient in political development? What roles do metaphor and oppositional categories play in explanatory frameworks? What are deemed to be the biggest threats to modernization and development? How are the obstacles to development to be overcome?

My second claim is that theories of modernization and dependency contain implications about issues beyond their explicit content and speak to issues that are marked by gender, although there are usually no explicit references to gender as a fundamental category of analysis. Those readers who are wedded to a deductive model of scientific inquiry will no doubt be uncomfortable with such an approach, because of the absence of a set of predetermined and specified questions that I systematically apply to an identifiable body of data in order to uncover relationships between variables. This study is more in the tradition of interpretive analysis, which often relies on the implicit and contextual meanings of texts—an effort that Brown (1988: 13–14) calls a "search 'beyond and beneath' theorists' utterances," an "archeological activity involved in grasping what lies under or to the side of explicit declarations by a theorist, grasping what makes the declaration important to the theorist as well as what makes it possible." To paraphrase Huntington (1987: 3), I am attempting to deconstruct the "theory about the thing [development]," especially through examination of "what is left out of the text, what is unnamed, what is excluded, what is concealed" (Rosenau 1992: 120). The ambivalent and powerfully charged opposition of feminized tradition with masculinized public life constitutes a significant underlying theme that informs a seemingly disparate body of literature about development, modernity, dependence, and revolution. My case is built around this less conventional practice of rereading, with the aim of persuading the reader that the interpretation is not only interesting or provocative, but convincing.

The texts I have chosen are only a part of the canon of modernization and dependency theory, but they constitute some of the most important work done in both fields. Following Randall and Theobald (1985: 15), Chapter 2 divides modernization theory into two approaches, the psychocultural and the structural-functional. I examine the work of Inkeles and Smith, Lerner, and McClelland as exemplars of the psycho-cultural approach. Rostow, Parsons, and the work of the Social Science Research Council's committee on comparative politics on crises and sequences of political development represent the structural approach. Hyden and other theorists who make claims about the softness of the African state are analyzed in Chapter 3. Soft-state theory's counterpart in World Bank policy is discussed in Chapter 4. Ruccio and Simon (1989) write about Frank and Amin as leaders of the radical school of dependency theory, along with the mode of production approach. In addition to Frank, Amin, and some representative texts that analyze the mode of production, Rodney is discussed in Chapter 5, as is Cardoso and Faletto. Chapter 6 examines the revolutionary politics aimed at challenging dependence. In conclusion, Chapter 7 contains suggestions about the importance of rereading and the prospects for rewriting development theory.

▲ Notes

1. Dependency theory, because of its Marxist heritage, has certainly been less hegemonic in the field of development studies, whereas the liberal, market-oriented, and anti-Communist animus of modernization theory helped to establish its power in development theory. However, I would argue that within the dependency theory there is a hegemonic consensus about the causes of underdevelopment and the need for revolution that has particular gendered meanings.

2. The exception is Inkeles and Smith (1974: 229), who argue that factories and schools rather than cities play a decisive role in modernization.

▲ 2
Tradition and Gender in Modernization Theory

There does not seem to be much more to write about modernization theory of the 1950s and 1960s. Numerous critics have taken early modernization theorists such as Rostow (1960), Parsons (1960), and Inkeles (1969) to task for their ethnocentrism, naive optimism, and "failure to recognize the political implications of economic dependency upon the West" (Randall and Theobald 1985: 33). Other critics pointed to modernization theory's reliance upon evolutionary and linear notions of social and political change and its reductionism and oversimplification of the development process (e.g., Portes 1976; Tipps 1976).[1] However, upon closer inspection it is evident that modernization theory was mainly criticized for its empirical content, lack of predictive ability, definitional shortcomings, and Western bias. Virtually no questions were asked about the way in which challenges to modernization were framed, and the extent to which the dichotomies of traditional and modern depended upon conceptions of gender, gender differences, and the devaluation of "the feminine."

Embedded within constructions of traditional society are ideas about women, family, and community that function as points of contrast for modernization theorists' idealization of a rational, forward-looking, male-dominated public sphere. Conceptions of linear time also play an important role for modernization theorists, with tradition and the feminine viewed as part of the past. As Inkeles and Smith (1974: 3–4) put it, "Mounting evidence suggests that it is impossible for a state to move into the twentieth century if its people continue to live in an earlier era." For development theorists seeking to construct the antinomy of tradition and modernity, it is important to distance one from the other and stress the importance of autonomy and separation of men from the household and the feminine traits associated with it.

There are three major themes evident in the work of theorists as diverse as Alex Inkeles and W. W. Rostow. The first is an unconscious and pervasive psychological preoccupation with separation and differentiation from the household. This distancing is accomplished by the presentation of tradition as a bundle of characteristics that also have historically been used to subordinate women and denigrate the social relations associated with females, especially mothers. It is interesting to note that some early critics of modernization theory argued that it undertheorized tradition and presented it as a static and "residual concept" (Randall and Theobald 1985: 35). This chapter will argue that the powerful imagery and the descriptions of idealized modernity provided by early modernization theorists were laden with such significant demarcations of constructed gender differences that explicit explorations of tradition were unnecessary.

A second theme evident in early modernization theory is the reliance on the public/private distinction in discussions of modernity and tradition. Modernity, rationality, technological progress, and good government are achieved in a public realm inhabited by autonomous men. With the exception of the Comparative Politics Committee of the Social Science Research Council (SSRC), which displayed some ambivalence toward tradition and called for more exploration of the content of traditional societies, early modernization theorists viewed tradition, and the values associated with tradition and women, as absolutely incompatible with modern institutions.

Finally, early modernization theorists rely, implicitly or explicitly, upon evolutionary models of social and political change, which provide an important lens for viewing their ideas about development, modernization, and gender. In their reliance upon an evolutionary model, they inevitably portray development as a struggle for dominance over nature, and implicitly, over women. Moreover, in using an evolutionary model, they portray development as the ever-widening ability of men to create and transform their environment. Within this linear framework of evolutionary social and political change, women are "left behind," confined to the household and denied citizenship. Women's continued subordination in fact defines male citizenship.

▲ Sexism and Modernization Theory

The argument here is that modernization theorists brought deeply held masculinist and dualistic views of the world of tradition and modernity that relied upon configurations of the public and private spheres, the household, and evolutionary progress. It is important and useful also to note that this literature consistently purported to present a universal model of the modernization process that was, in fact, partial and based on an (often idealized) version of masculine modernity. Women are either invisible, treated paternalistically, or used as a litmus test for determining the degree of "backwardness" of a particular Third World country. A startling example of invisibility is the project that interviewed six thousand men in Argentina, Chile, East Pakistan (Bangladesh), India, Israel, and Nigeria in order to examine the effects of factory life on modern attitudes (Inkeles 1969; Inkeles and Smith 1974). They report that budget limitations and the concentration of men in industrial jobs explain the gender of the sample (Inkeles and Smith 1974: 311). But, surely, would not women be included in the cultivator and nonindustrial worker category, two other categories of respondents interviewed in each of the countries? The authors never explain why only men were included in these categories as well. They also make the interesting assertion, "We are firmly convinced that the overwhelming majority of the psychosocial indicators we used to identify the modern man would also discriminate effectively among women" (Inkeles, Smith, et al. 1983: 123). This directly contradicts their reporting on the low correlations concerning modern attitudes about political life and attitudes about the family.

As an example of striking paternalism, Daniel Lerner (1958: 29) took Zilla K. along as an interviewer when he returned to the village of Balgat, Turkey, in 1954 (he had been there four years before). This is his description of her hiring:

> I had "ordered" her through a colleague, at Ankara University, "by the numbers": thirtyish, semi-trained, alert, compliant with instructions, not sexy enough to impede our relations with the men of Balgat but chic enough to provoke the women. A glance and a word showed that Zilla filled the requisition.

Rostow (1960: 91) speculated about what lies beyond the state of high mass-consumption reached by societies such as the United States and worried about the onset of pervasive boredom—for men. Women, on the other hand, "will not recognize the reality of the problem" because of their involvement in childrearing: "The problem of boredom is a man's problem, at least until the children have grown up."

The comparison of the liberated and independent woman of the West with the tradition-bound woman of the Third World also informs many accounts of the psychosocial requisites of modernity. When women are discussed by the modernization theorists in any specific way they are presented in remarkably flat terms, and often uniformly oppressed by men and family structures. Lerner (1958: 199) notes that "traditional women are content to accept the role and status assigned them," as the "stolid guardians of custom and routine." Women who represent modern values in Middle Eastern societies such as Lebanon yearn for the greater educational and career opportunities available to women in the West. The Western media provides a constant reminder to Middle Eastern women of their restricted opportunities. In a puzzling analogy, Lerner (1958: 204) notes that "as the American housewife uses soap operas to fill her day and satisfy her needs, so this young Lebanese woman finds gratification through borrowed experiences." While implicitly acknowledging that viewing soap operas might represent frustration and denied opportunities for middle-class U.S. women, Lerner never explicitly challenges the media's juxtaposition of the "enlightened and independent woman" of the West with the backward and traditional woman of the Middle East. McClelland (1976: 399–400) makes a similar contrast:

> A crucial way to break with tradition and introduce new norms is via the emancipation of women. . . . The most general explanation lies in the fact that women are the most conservative members of a culture. They are less subject to influences outside the home than the men and yet they are the ones who rear the next generation and give it the traditional values of the culture.

Inkeles and Smith, et al. describe "most of the traditional societies and communities of the world" as "if not strictly patriarchal, at least vigorously male dominated" (Inkeles and Smith, et al. 1983: 26). While traditional man is reluctant to accept women's freedom, modern man is willing to "allow women to take advantage of opportunities outside the confines of the household" (Inkeles and Smith 1974: 77, 291). In a later work they predicted that "the liberating forces of modernization would act on men's attitudes and incline them to accord to women status and rights more nearly equal to those enjoyed by men" (Inkeles, Smith, et al. 1983: 42). Such contrasts not only serve to establish a Western sense of difference and superiority (and complacency about women's rights in the West); they also mark women, in Mohanty's (1991b: 56) terms, as "third world (read: ignorant, poor, uneducated, tradition-bound, domestic, family-oriented, victimized, etc.)." As the most "backward" group in society, women serve as an implicit contrast between Western modernity and non-Western tradition.

▲ **"Becoming Modern":**
The Syndrome of Modern Male Citizenship

Randall and Theobald (1985: 15) place early modernization theories into one of two categories: psychocultural or structural-functional.

Psychocultural approaches examine the attitudinal prerequisites of modernity, while structural-functional approaches focus on the institutional changes needed for modernity. Inkeles (1969), Inkeles and Smith (1974), and Inkeles, Smith, et al. (1983) adopt a psychocultural approach to modernization. In the study of six thousand men in the six countries listed above, Inkeles and Smith locate a syndrome of participant citizenship, "attitudes and capacities" necessary to realize "nation-building and institution-building" in the Third World (1974: 3).

Inkeles and Smith (1974: 19–24) argue that twelve traits define modern man (sic). In addition, they argue that modernity is also characterized by a host of other orientations toward religion, the family, and social stratification (1974: 25). Their analytic and topical characteristics of the modern man are summarized in Table 2.1. Feminist critics of the Western philosophical tradition have noted the persistent denigration of the feminine within that tradition. Lloyd (1984: 2–3), for example, notes that in the triumph of reason over darkness, the early Greeks used symbolic associations of the female as what needed "to be shed in developing culturally prized rationality." Rooney (1991: 91) and Jordanova (1980) have noted the images of battle or struggle that are common in discussions of reason and unreason. Jordanova's (1980: 44) presentation of the dichotomies that emerged in the biomedical sciences in the eighteenth and nineteenth centuries showed similarities with the contrasts between traditional and modern man presented by Inkeles and Smith (see Table 2.1).

Table 2.1   Eighteenth- and Nineteenth-Century Dichotomies

Traditional	Modern
Nature	Culture
Woman	Man
Physical	Mental
Mothering	Thinking
Feeling and superstition	Abstract knowledge and thought
Country	City
Darkness	Light
Nature	Science and civilization

Source: Jordanova 1980: 44

Jordanova (1980: 44) suggests that the oppositions contain an important gender dimension and connotations of battle: the struggle between the forces of tradition and modernity was also a struggle between the sexes, with the increasing assertion of masculinity over

"irrational, backward-looking women" applauded as inevitable. Furthermore, she shows how science and medicine used sexual
metaphors that portrayed nature as a woman to be penetrated, un-
clothed, and unveiled by masculine science (Jordanova 1980: 45).

Inkeles and Smith replicate these Enlightenment dichotomies in
their comparison of traditional and modern men (see Table 2.2). In
the larger study, they present case studies from East Pakistan
(Bangladesh) of a traditional man and a modern one (Inkeles and
Smith 1974: 73–80). Ahmadullah, the traditional man, "was relatively
passive, even fatalistic, and very much dependent on outside forces,
above all on the intervention of God." He said he could do nothing
in the face of an unjust law, and he preferred living in the "closed
and unchanging world" of the village. Nuril, on the other hand, had
lived in the city for ten years, approved of women acquiring more education, was open to meeting new people and having new experiences, and believed that "the outcome of things depended very
much on himself, and [that] others bore responsibility for their individual actions." As Inkeles noted in his earlier study (1969:
1122–1123), the modern man possesses an orientation toward politics that recognizes the necessity and desirability of a "rational structure of rules and regulations."

Juxtaposed with the village, family, and kinship structures stands
the factory, a "school in rationality" (Inkeles 1969: 1140). The factory is an exemplar of efficiency, innovation, planning, punctuality,
rules and formal procedures, and objective standards for assessing
skills and output (Inkeles and Smith 1974: 158–163). City life, they
argued, also has a powerful indirect effect on creating modern attitudes because cities have greater concentrations of schools, factories,
and mass media (Inkeles and Smith 1974: 228).

In addition to an uncritical perspective on the nature of factory
work in both the First and Third Worlds, the description by Inkeles
and Smith of the benefits of factory work rely upon a liberal framework of contractual obligation and individualism that reflects a masculinist standpoint and preoccupation with autonomy. Hirschmann
(1989: 1237) argues that this is especially evident in symbolic language that reflects desires for dominance and nonreciprocal recognition. In describing modern man's experiences as a "shift from the
more traditional settings of village, farm, and tribe to city residence,
industrial employment, and national citizenship" (Inkeles and
Smith 1974: 156), psychocultural theorists of modernization juxtapose community, family, and kinship with the modern, and it is
women who stand at the center of the traditional community. The
factory serves as the emblem of scientific progress and technological prowess that promises to shatter any resistance to rationalized

relationships in the public realm. This liberal and masculinist conception of freedom entails nonrecognition of the female and the relationships she represents. Freedom requires not only moving beyond the household: subordination of the household becomes the means of achieving freedom (Hirschmann 1989: 1235). Women were not only excluded from the samples because they worked in factories, but because they resided in the very location that undermines the institutions that "train men in active citizenship" (Inkeles 1969: 1141).

Table 2.2 Traditional Man and Modern Man

Traditional	Modern
Not receptive to new ideas	Open to new experience
Rooted in tradition	Change orientation
Only interested in things that touch him immediately	Interested in outside world
Denial of different opinions	Acknowledges different opinions
Uninterested in new information	Eager to seek out new information
Oriented toward the past	Punctual; oriented toward the present
Concerned with the short term	Values planning
Distrustful of people beyond the family	Calculability; trust in people to meet obligations
Suspicious of technology	Values technical skills
High value placed on religion and the sacred	High value placed on formal education and science
Traditional patron-client relations prevail	Respect for the dignity of others; belief that rewards should be distributed according to rules
Particularistic	Universalistic
Fatalistic	Optimistic

Source: Inkeles and Smith 1974: 19–34.

Daniel Lerner's *The Passing of Traditional Society* (1958) is another representative of the psychocultural approach. Lerner presents the parable of modern Turkey through the story of the Grocer and the Chief, two men interviewed in the village of Balgat, near Ankara, in 1950 and 1954. The Chief "was a man of few words on many subjects," who "audits his life placidly, makes no comparisons, thanks God." The Grocer, on the other hand, perceived his story as "a drama of self versus village," a man whose "psychic antennae were endlessly seeking the new future here and now" (Lerner 1958: 22, 24).

Lerner's contrasts between traditional and modern society (1958: 44) echo Enlightenment thinkers and Inkeles and Smith: "village versus town, land versus cash, illiteracy versus enlightenment, resignation versus ambition, piety versus excitement." In modern societies, personal mobility is a "first-order value," and a modern society "has to encourage rationality, for the calculus of choice shapes individual behavior and conditions its reward" (Lerner 1958: 48). Empathy is the mechanism that accompanies the transformation of traditional man, i.e., "the capacity to see oneself in the other fellow's situation" (Lerner 1958: 50). Empathy takes place through both projection ("assigning the object certain preferred attributes of the self") and introjection ("attributing to the self certain desirable attributes of the object") (Lerner 1958: 49). Identification with others is a key component of modern man's personality.

Chodorow has noted the importance of negative identification, differentiation, and nonrecognition in human development, and these themes recur in Lerner's definition of modern man's development and "maturation." Differentiation is defined relationally, and because men have "conflictual core gender identity problems," it is important to maintain a rigid boundary between the masculine and feminine: "Boys and men come to deny the feminine identification within themselves and those feelings they experience as feminine; feelings of dependence, relational needs, emotions generally" (1989: 109–110). The development of masculine identity as outlined by object relations theory resonates in Lerner's (1958: 410) definition of modern man's solitary struggle against forces represented by the village, "the passive, destitute, illiterate and altogether 'submerged' mass which looms so large in its [the Middle East's] sociological landscape."

McClelland's (1976: 107) chief goal was to determine the extent to which a "culture or nation has adapted more or less rapidly to modern civilization, with its stress on technology, the specialization of labor, and the factory system." McClelland and his colleagues developed a measure of "n achievement" (shorthand for need achievement) through content analysis of achievement-related stories written by male college students, folk tales from various cultures, and children's stories. He explicitly links high n achievement with boys who had mothers who encouraged independence yet at the same time provided warmth and affection. Reporting on earlier findings that attempted to demonstrate a link between socialization and the propensity for high achievement, McClelland (1976: 46) summarized: "The mothers of the sons with high n-achievement have set higher standards for their sons; they expect self-mastery at an early age." Thus he not only touches on themes within object relations theory, he literally claims that characteristics of mothering (along with other factors) are influential in determining whether a society develops. McClelland (1976: 404–495) also warns about father-dominance in producing low achievement, because "the boy is more likely to get his conception of the male role from his relationship with the father rather than his mother and therefore, to conceive of himself as a dependent, obedient sort of person if his father is strong and dominating" (McClelland 1976: 353). It is in his relationship with the mother that the boy obtains a sense of independence and autonomy, but only from mothers who are "controlled and moderate in warmth and affection" (McClelland 1976: 405).

From these observations, McClelland hypothesizes about how to bring about development. First, "other-directedness" is essential (McClelland 1976: 192). The "authority of tradition" must be replaced and men must learn to pay attention to newspapers, local political parties, and the radio, a "new voice of authority." Development, in other words, requires a shift in allegiance from the private to the public realm. Second, n achievement needs to be increased, and McClelland speculates about the prospects for decreasing father-dominance, protestant conversion, and a reorganization of fantasy life (McClelland 1976: 406–418). Finally, McClelland suggests that existing n achievement resources could be used more efficiently to encourage "young men with high n achievement to turn their talents to business or productive enterprise" (McClelland 1976: 418).

Rostow's (1960) *Stages of Economic Growth* introduces both the concept of evolutionary stages of societal development and attitudinal prerequisites as crucial for understanding political development. He conceptualizes the evolutionary path of development as composed of five stages: tradition, societies poised to "take-off," the "take-off" into modernity itself, the drive to maturity, and the age of high mass-consumption. Traditional societies are characterized by Rostow (1960: 4) as "pre-Newtonian" because they are located on the other side of "that watershed in history when men came widely to believe that the external world was subject to a few knowable laws and was capable of productive manipulation." The "frame of mind" conducive to modern science was nonexistent in these pre-Newtonian societies, which possessed a "long-term fatalism" and a "ceiling on the productivity of their economic techniques" (Rostow 1960: 5). During the time before take-off, "limited bursts" of entrepreneurial activity and "enclaves of modernity" emerge, spurred by "enterprising men" who are willing to "take risks in pursuit of profit or modernization" (Rostow 1960: 6–7). Rostow presents us with the image of energetic men emerging from rural backwardness and leaving the bonds of tradition to transform and manipulate the forces of nature:

> Man need not regard his physical environment as virtually a given factor by nature and providence, but as an ordered world which, if rationally understood, can be manipulated in ways which yield

productive change and, in one dimension at least, progress (1960: 19).

Rostow contrasts the world of family, mother, and household with the modern world of markets, technology, and science. In fact, traditional societies become eligible for take-off when "men come to be valued in society not with their connection with clan or class . . . but for their individual ability to perform certain specific, increasingly specialized functions" (Rostow 1960: 19). This requires attitudinal changes toward science, propensities to calculate and take risks, and a willingness to work (Rostow 1960: 20). Rostow appeals to male heroic leadership in his analysis of the key take-off from tradition to modernity. He juxtaposes this new elite with "the old land-based elite" which is mired in agrarian practices and worldviews that do not regard "modernization as a possible task" (Rostow 1960: 26).

▲ Equality, Capacity, and Differentiation: Structural Explanations of Modernity

Structural-functional frameworks for explaining modernization and development share the dualistic and gendered framework employed by psychocultural approaches. Parsons' pattern-variables of universal social roles represent the most famous structural-functional approach (Parsons 1960). Parsons makes distinctions between affectively neutral and affective actions, universal and particular orientations, specific and diffuse obligations, self-oriented rather than collectively oriented behavior, and achievement and ascriptive criteria for recognizing performance, with modernity characterizing the first category in each paired concept. In addition to opposing tradition and modernity in this way, Parsons also unconsciously "feminizes" traditional society in that the terms he uses to define "traditional" Third World societies have also been used to juxtapose male rationality and inherent superiority with "lower order" female passions and instincts.

One of Parsons's most interesting distinctions is between universal and particular modes of categorizing social objects. While modern man is able to use a set of norms and standards that apply to all objects in a particular class, traditional man treats them in terms of their standing in some particular relationship to him (Bluh 1982: 88–90). As Devereaux (1961: 41) explains it,

Whether someone is a good doctor, a competent secretary, or a beautiful woman are presumably matters to be determined on universalistic grounds. But while certain modes of behavior might be evoked toward beautiful women or deserving children in general, where one's own wife or child is involved, one is committed in many special ways, regardless of beauty or desert.

Parsons (1960: 119) identifies the major obstacles to economic development as a "combination of 'traditionalism' and a strong pressure to reproduce the existing pattern of economic organization wherever opportunity exists for its expansion." Developed societies, on the other hand, have legal systems that embody principles of universalism and specificity, contracts and property, and occupational roles that free individuals "from ties and imperatives which would interfere seriously with economic production" (Parsons 1960: 147).

While Parsons is obviously enumerating the values and institutions compatible with capitalist development, he is also denigrating characteristics of traditional societies that have historically been associated with women and devalued in the Western tradition. The individual's quest for modernity is a battle against the village, family, and "tribe." These communities are not only averse to economic productivity and the capitalist work ethic; they represent, symbolically, female attributes and the relationships and structures historically associated with them.

Parsons (1964: 356) also relied explicitly upon an evolutionary model of development. He argued that certain "organizational complexes" were necessary for societies to emerge from "primitiveness." In order to evolve along the scale of development, societies require stratification, necessary to emerge from the "seamless web" of relationships that characterize societies governed by strong kinship and family ties (Parsons 1964: 342). Stratification is necessary in order to create avenues of upward mobility for leaders who wish to marshal the resources for development (Parsons 1964: 34). Extending this functionalist and evolutionary framework even further, Parsons argues that legitimation is necessary in order to justify hierarchy; bureaucracy is necessary in order to develop enhanced capacity for change; money and markets are necessary as "the great mediator of the instrumental use of goods and services" (Parsons 1964: 349).

Parsons makes a number of key assumptions in this presentation of evolutionary development. He assumes that power must be concentrated in hierarchies of stratification in order for political development to occur. Kinship and family ties, on the other hand, are clearly "rigid" and incapable of generating power to effect change. Second, Parsons assumes that development will be a divisive process, as one group will inevitably seek power and try to achieve dominance over another. He never doubts that struggles and drives for dominance

will increase the "long-run adaptive capacity" of societies evolving toward the development ideal (Parsons 1964: 340). He assumes that
despite "severe dislocations" resulting from such struggles, the societies undergoing evolutionary development are experiencing an inevitable and "natural" process. Why is stratification necessary in order
to marshal resources? Why is a concentration of power necessary for
productive change to take place? While Parsons produces a legitimation of capitalism and markets, he also implicitly presents male/cul-
ture triumphant over female/nature. The evolutionary universals
considered fundamental for understanding development are also jus-
tifications for male dominance and denigration of traits historically
associated with women. Liberal ideology and evolutionary functionalism join together to legitimate masculinist individualism and domination and exclusionary practices with regard to the household.

The SSRC Committee on Comparative Politics also worked with
a structural-functional framework. They located a "development syndrome" as increasing equality, capacity, and differentiation, the evolution of which produces inevitable strains and tensions in traditional and transitional societies. They defined the obstacles to the
achievement of development as "crises" of identity, legitimacy, participation, penetration, and distribution, faced by every society in
"building both state and nation" (Pye 1971a: viii). Coleman (1971:
73) pointed out that the SSRC participants chose to view development as an evolutionary process—as an

> open-ended increase in the capacity of political man to initiate and
> institutionalize new structures and supporting cultures, to cope
> with or resolve problems, to absorb and adapt to continuous
> change, and to strive purposively and creatively for the attainment
> of new goals.

The SSRC committee characterized development and modernization
as conflictual processes laden with the potential for setbacks. While a
"complete reversion to a traditional pre-modern system" had not yet
occurred, there had been "abortive developments" in many Third
World countries (Coleman 1971: 84). In fact, Coleman (1971: 100)
argued that "arrested development" may begin to affect an increasing number of Third World countries as they became stalled at a certain level of differentiation, equality, and capacity.

Abortive or arrested development occurs as a result of conflicts
in the resolution of the five "crises" listed above. For example, fragmentation challenges state capacity for integration; demands for
equality challenge the state's ability to solve the participation crisis;
challenges to state capacity create legitimacy and identity crises, and

so forth. As Pye (1971b: 106) notes, these crises, if unresolved, create difficulties in achieving a "higher level of performance" on the part of Third World leaders. Pye's (1971b: 110) discussion of the identity crisis is especially worth noting. He argues that identity crises take place over four different issues: territory, class, ethnicity, and social change. In a revealing discussion of the legacy of colonialism, Pye (1971b: 122) discusses the ambivalence these leaders feel toward colonial relationships of dependence:

> All humans must experience complete and protracted dependency, for it is the very mark of human-ness. . . . With development people have ambivalent feelings toward their sentiments related to dependency, and the search for individual identity inevitably involves an assertion for independence in which any continuing cravings for dependence must be veiled.

These themes, which resemble theories of male psychological development, recur throughout the SSRC committee's discussion of modernization and development. Anxiety, crises, capacity, performance, individual identity, and overcoming the challenges posed by tradition represent the "syndrome" of development in both becoming a mature male adult and a mature, national society.

Furthermore, modernization is conceived as a masculine triumph, the result of enhanced capacity, improved performance, and effective penetration. La Palombara (1971: 206) conceives of the crisis of penetration as a "test" of the "organizational, technological, and/or diplomatic capabilities of an existing governing elite." It refers to "whether [leaders] can get what they want from people over whom they seek to exercise power" (La Palombara 1971: 209). Gaining compliance, creating new organizations, and breaking down old loyalties are all aspects of the penetration challenge.

Reliance on an evolutionary model of modernization is also evident in the SSRC committee's work (Coleman 1971: 75). Images of struggle are deeply embedded in evolutionary models of society that emerged in the nineteenth century. Gross and Averill (1983: 81) note that the importance of competition in evolutionary theory was used by men in the twentieth century to impose order on the perceived chaos associated with reproduction:

> Evolution and natural selection, as products of nineteenth century thought, coincide with other reflections of men's anxiety about women, most plainly displayed in their preoccupation with her reproductive ability: her uncontrolled sexuality, her ("pathological") reproductive physiology, even her (hysterical) psychology. The nineteenth century medicalization of women's reproductive capacities . . . parallels the emphasis on domination and competition in

nature as the main restraints over unbridled chaos in the orderly evolution of species.

Structural-functional theories of evolutionary development can also be viewed as expressing masculine concern and preoccupation with the fragmentation, particularism, and even chaos of traditional society. The modernization process is laden with conflict, a "ceaseless straining and tugging between the development processes and the requirement that the political system maintain itself" (Pye 1971b: 101). Assumptions that "abortive" or "arrested" development are inevitable and demand specialization, hierarchy, and enhanced capacity in order for progress to take place, constitute a masculinist version of modernity and development.

The view of development as an evolutionary struggle to achieve greater capacity to dominate nature coincides with the liberal underpinnings of modernization theory, which also relies upon assumptions of scarcity. In Macpherson's phrase, liberalism makes a "maximizing claim" (1973: 4) in that it provides a framework for realizing individual desires. Modernization theory shares this view of humans as "essentially a bundle of appetites demanding satisfaction." Macpherson (1973: 18–19) argues that liberal theory pits unlimited desire against scarcity, with unlimited desire conceived of as rational and morally acceptable rather than deplored as greed: "the chief purpose of man is an endless battle against scarcity" (Macpherson 1973: 18). Evolutionary paradigms of development also assume that "scarcity is inevitable and in turn demands competition, which is expressed in dominance relationships that make for evolutionary 'progress'" (Gross and Averill 1983: 82).

▲ Modernization Revisionists

The initial criticisms of modernization theory came from theorists who continued to characterize modernity and tradition in dualistic terms, but who insisted on the recognition of the continuing salience of caste, ethnicity, and other "particularistic" characteristics of traditional societies. Rudolph and Rudolph, for example, pointed to the resilience of caste organizations in Indian politics, adhered to the meaning of tradition and modernity held by earlier theorists:

> Modernity assumes that local ties and parochial perspectives give way to universal commitments and cosmopolitan attitudes; the truths of utility, calculation, and science take precedence over those of the emotions, the sacred, and the non-rational . . . that mastery rather than fatalism orient their attitude toward the material and human environment (1967: 3–4).

In addition, theories about patrimonialism and the "soft state" reinforced the appreciation of traditional institutions and represented a departure from early modernization theory because they challenged the assumption that Western institutions could be duplicated in postcolonial societies. Samuel Huntington also challenged the naive optimism of modernization theorists.

▲ Creating a (Gendered) Political Order

Samuel Huntington's *Political Order in Changing Societies* (1968) attempted to temper the optimism of modernization theorists by pointing to the potential problems that could occur during the modernization process. *Political Order* opens with a Manichaean vision of international politics (1968: 1). On one side of the divide are modern polities such as the United States, Great Britain, and the Soviet Union, with their "effective bureaucracies, well-organized political parties . . . and reasonably effective procedures for regulating succession and controlling political conflict." On the other side there are the governments of Asia, Africa, and Latin America, where "increasing ethnic and class conflict, recurring rioting and mob violence, frequent military coup d'état . . . the loss of authority by legislatures and courts" constitute the norms of public life. Modernization theory, Huntington argues, could not anticipate this outcome because it assumed that economic development and social mobilization would lead to political development. Huntington (1968: 41) argued that the very process of modernization threatened the political order. Thus the task of developing countries should be to create political institutions that "derive their interests not from the extent to which they represent the interests of the people or any other group but the extent to which they have distinct interests of their own apart from other groups" (1968: 27). Like modernization theorists, Huntington argues that political institutions must attain autonomy, but he presents the achievement of autonomy as a struggle that must be waged against the confusion, chaos, and alienation that accompany modernization (1968: 30–31). Order must be created: "Men may, of course, have order without liberty, but they cannot have liberty without order" (1968: 7–8).

Huntington takes a grim view of the world of politics. In defending his calls for order in societies with weak institutions, he writes that "politics is a Hobbesian world of unrelenting competition of social forces—between man and man, family and family, clan and clan, region and region, class and class—a competition unmediated by more comprehensive political organizations" (1968: 24). He implies that modernizing societies lack the kind of rationality required to

38 Gender and Development

create political institutions to regulate conflict and that a government ordered along the lines of the military is most likely to create
viable political institutions:

> Unity, esprit, morale, and discipline are needed in governments as
> well as regiments. . . . The problems of creating coherent political
> organizations are more difficult but not fundamentally different
> from those involved in the creation of coherent military organiza-
> tions. . . . Discipline and development go hand in hand (1968:
> 33–34).

Huntington's dualistic brand of thinking, his endorsement of authoritarian government, and his praise for the coherence and discipline of military modes of governance make his work one of the
most remarkable and striking in development theory and perhaps
suggest a reason for the wide appeal and readership of the book. His
formulation of the challenges of development also have a distinctively masculinist tenor. For Huntington, the ends of politics should
be toward creating political institutions that, once in place, are capable of regulating political conflicts that arise (1968: 9, 11). In
proposing his well-run polity with coherent, adaptable, autonomous,
and complex political institutions, he explicitly contrasts the world of
"natural" communities, "the isolated clan, family, or tribe," with political institutions and organizations that are consciously created
through "political action" and "political labor" (1968: 10–11). "Natural" communities are simple, spontaneous, and less diverse; political communities are man-made political structures that do not de-
pend upon the obligations and relationships that exist in "natural"
communities. They are based on purely instrumental and calculating
imperatives. Furthermore, Huntington's emphasis upon teamwork,
command, and discipline, and his analogy between creating coherent political organizations and coherent military structures reflect a
distinctly heroic, atomistic, and individualistic approach to governance. While earlier modernization theorists conceived of tradition
and the socially constructed feminine values associated with it as
something to be transcended, Huntington views it as a dangerous
force to be tamed and disciplined.

Huntington is a transitional figure in development theory. He
made his case for a politics of order by challenging the naïve belief
in evolutionary progress exhibited by many earlier modernization
theorists of the early 1960s. Dependency theorists reacted against
Huntington's call for order and his neglect of international politics
and economics in affecting political stability in the Third World. The
continuing power of modernization theory's frame of reference (including Huntington) in contemporary theorizing about African politics is explored in the next chapter.

▲ Conclusion

Early modernization theory has been discredited for being unscientific and sexist in its focus on male heads of households. While these are valid criticisms, it is also important to examine the implicit assumptions, concerns, unstated preoccupations, and avoidances of these early theorists. Despite its official demise, early modernization theory's conceptual foundations continue to have pervasive power. This power helps explain the difficulty encountered by those who seek to challenge its masculinist worldview.

There is no need to speculate about the early upbringing of these male theorists to recognize the links they make between traditional society, on the one hand, and the denial of power and autonomy for the household and women, on the other. As Hirschmann (1989: 1232) notes, if self-conceptions are gender-related, accompanying worldviews will also differ by gender. And as Flax (1983: 246) contends, "patriarchy by definition imputes political, moral, and social *meanings* to sexual differentiation." Object relations theory provides a powerful means for understanding the themes of differentiation, autonomy, identity, and suppression of the household's characteristics that play so heavily in modernization theory. For these theorists, modernization requires self-propelled men to leave the household, abandon tradition, and assume their rightful place among other rational men. Women and the household are conceived of as part of the past that contains the dangerous worldview that nature is unalterable and that man is powerless in his efforts to control it. Only the SSRC committee displayed a hint of ambivalence about the compatibility of traditional and modern institutions. Coleman (171: 86–89) argued that, at times, traditional institutions can facilitate modernization, but only to the extent that traditional society has some characteristics that resemble the modern one! This is rarely the case, according to modernization theory, as traditional societies are composed of "highly pluralistic traditions that reflect very different, frequently conflicting or incongruent cultural patterns" (Coleman 1971: 87). Societies are modern to the extent that they overcome tradition, but abortive or arrested development are constant possibilities. Being "stuck" on the evolutionary scale toward national maturity reflects anxiety over the ability of state leaders to resolve their ambivalence toward dependence. Modernization is the triumph of penetration, identity, and legitimation, and the subordination of tradition, nature, and the "feminine."

Theories of modernization also replicate the public/private split that has occupied such a prominent place in Western political thought. It is a complicated tradition that at times has treated the private sphere and females as inferior and derivative and at other times complementary to the "male paradigm of excellence" (Lloyd 1984: 75). Modernization theory does not present tradition and the household as a different type of rationality that possesses its own form of excellence. Inkeles and Smith and others judge all traditional societies against the idealized standard of (male) rationality, universal norms, and achievement criteria. Tradition always fails to meet these standards and in fact its persistence threatens the public life of male citizenship. The dichotomous comparisons of traditional and modern man made by Inkeles and Smith are almost a caricature of Enlightenment dichotomies that portrayed tradition as embodying ignorant peasant women tenaciously clinging to kin and family in the face of the benevolent progress offered by technology and science.

Finally, it is important to note that the themes of struggle and mastery over idealized and feminized tradition dovetail with a liberal conception of society, functionalism, evolutionary metaphors, and the possibility of human engineering in development. Haraway (1978: 26) defines human engineering as "the project of design and management of human material for efficient, rational functioning in a scientifically organized society." Parsons' audacious attempt to pinpoint the necessary societal functions for the emergence from "primitiveness," the "seamless web" of kinship and clan, is a classic example of the wholesale adoption of a Darwinian framework of social change to human societies. Images of struggle and surging toward the achievement of a "break through" (Parsons 1964: 357) from the morass of tradition and the chaos of the household permeate Parsons' theory and modernization theory generally. The only way to achieve "adaptive capacity" is to deny tradition. Evolution as a cultural product serves to justify industrial capitalism and the subordination of women. It serves a similar function in theories of modernization.

There has been a resurgence of interest in the study of tradition in development theory, for a number of reasons. In general, assertion of ethnic and "primordial" sentiments and the role of culture and values in the East Asian "economic miracles" has led to an appreciation of the continuing importance of tradition as both obstacle and facilitator of development (Banuazizi 1987: 284). In African studies, the failure of Afro-Marxist regimes and the reign of structural adjustment programs from the World Bank and International Monetary Fund (IMF) have led to a "profound period of revisionism" (Shaw 1991: 193). Africa's continued marginal position in the international division of labor has led to a search for explanations that ostensibly go beyond theories of modernization and dependence. However, a significant body of this theory constitutes an attempt to revive modernization theory's gendered dichotomies. The next chapter will show how theories of the African "soft state" seek to demonstrate the extent to which the characteristics of traditional/feminine society have become predominant in state practices. For theorists of the "soft state," the task of modernization is not only that of ridding society of its tradition, softness, and "femininity," but also that of similarly changing the state: the modern state is the hardened, masculine state.

▲ Note

1. The role of the Cold War in shaping U.S. development theory and practice is explored in different ways by Packenham (1973) and Gendzier (1985).

▲ 3
From Modernization Theory to the "Soft State" in Africa

The theoretical foci of development theory began to shift in the 1970s and 1980s in order to take into account the different development patterns that appeared to be taking shape in the Third World. Debates emerged about the so-called East Asian miracles in Taiwan, South Korea, and Singapore (see, e.g., Chan 1987). In Latin America, renewed focus on the state and transitions from military rule to civilian pluralist democracy received a great deal of attention. In Africa, on the other hand, debates about the utility of development theory had ground nearly to a halt and had been overshadowed by alarming prognostications about impending catastrophe. Industrial production in Africa relative to East Asian economies had declined in the 1980s; the export of manufactured goods was miniscule when compared with East Asian economies (Mittelman 1991: 92). To Nyang'oro (1989: 1), the phrase that captured Africa's "deteriorating economic and political conditions" had become "continent in crisis." *Stagnation, decline,* and *impending catastrophe* were words used regularly by Africans and Western theorists to describe the state of every aspect of the economy from food production to industry. Although the 1975 independence of the former Portuguese colonies, preceded by years of guerrilla struggle, looked promising, those governments were confronted with counterrevolutionary movements and other challenges in the creation of sustained revolutionary politics. For many theorists, neither modernization theory nor dependency theory offered a reliable framework for understanding Africa's political economy.

Goran Hyden's work needs to be placed in this context. His theoretical approach to the African state has been used by various scholars: by those who challenged the utility of categorizing African regimes into African capitalist, African socialist, and Afro-Communist (Scott 1988); by anthropologists who argued for the continued resilience of informal networks in African societies (Waters 1992); and in a whole spate of research published on voluntary associations and civil society in Africa in the 1980s and 1990s (Rothchild and Chazan 1988). Mamdani (1985), Samatar and Samatar (1987), and Hyden and Peters (1991) have criticized Hyden on the grounds that his work represents a refashioning of modernization theory, but they have confined their discussions largely to issues such as his characterizations of the material life of the African peasantry. No one has explored the underlying constructions of gender relied upon by Hyden and other Africanists concerned with "weakening civic capacity" (Wunsh and Olowu 1990: 5).

Women are usually invisible in Hyden's work except, significantly, in a table he presents on the "basic features of the economy of affection as applied to female-headed households in Kenya" (Hyden 1983a: 16). Hyden does not ponder whether the economy of affection is a gender-specific activity. This is in some ways paradoxical, because his entire approach relies upon well-established social constructions of gender differences and the validation of one set at the expense of another. This representation is evident even in his first full-length account of the "soft state," *Beyond Ujamaa* (1980), where he juxtaposes modern-and-big with small-but-powerful. Modern-and-big refers to colonial and postcolonial unsuccessful attempts to capture the small-but-powerful peasantry in a permanent relationship with the state. The titles of the chapters convey images of the small-but-powerful hiding, deceiving, infiltrating, and finally pervading state institutions, a view of the peasantry that relies on socially constructed dualisms that have pervaded Western treatments of "essential" female attributes for centuries. This chapter will explore the emergence of the concept of the "soft state" in Gunnar Myrdal's work and its revival by Hyden in the 1980s. It traces the influence of this approach in the field and suggests that the reason for its prominence lies in the implicit and gendered oppositions it proposes. Ideas about the public realm, masculinist insecurity, preoccupations with challenges, heroic leadership, and buoyant faith in linear progress and science all explain the continued hold of modernization theory and its offspring, soft-state theory, in the study of African political economy.

▲ State and Society in Africa

Efforts to "bring the state back in" (Skoçpol 1985) and "return to the state" (Almond 1988) have been taken up with great enthusiasm by Africanists, many of whom have portrayed the African state as a "lame Leviathan," incapable of meeting the challenges of ethnic conflict, facing threats from the military, or implementing new economic policies (Fatton 1989a: 171). With few exceptions, most conceptualizations of the state in Africa explore what Mitchell (1991: 82) terms "the formation and expression of authoritative intentions" of state leaders, a rendering of the state as an anthropomorphized entity with aspirations to achieve independence from and establish dominance over society. Much of the statist literature lapses into an idealization of a personified state invested with subjectivity and agency as it attempts to maintain insularity from social forces. This helps explain why much of the literature of the 1980s reads like an advice manual to an imaginary African prince: African leaders are advised to display discipline, wield effective authority, and bolster their capacity. This tendency to treat the state an an organization of leaders and officials independent of society is within the Weberian tradition of viewing state and society as marked by definite boundaries which are shored up by state leaders and used to maintain order and mobilize resources (Skoçpol 1985: 9). Jackson and Rosberg (1982: 77) provide a vivid example of this voluntarist analysis of the state: "Whether abusive rule or constructive forms of personal rulership are practiced in a country depends less on underlying social conditions and more on *political actors* who must govern without institutions to assist them" (my emphasis).

Hyden and other theorists of the African state rely on a model that poses it as "an originary subjective entity composed of individual preferences, thoughts, decisions, and other ideational phenomena— a person writ large" (Mitchell 1991: 83). While theorizing about the African state is often accompanied by historically situated analysis— characterizations that usually treat the state as premodern, patrimonial, and "soft"—it fails to examine the role of the state in class formation, maintaining a pact of domination, or establishing ideologies of rule. Rather, "creative statecraft" is presented as the key challenge facing African leaders in their efforts to "politically manage" society's demands (Bratton and Rothchild 1992: 264, 274).

▲ The Asian "Soft State"

Despite the new emphasis upon the elasticity of tradition and hints about the potential usefulness of traditional institutions for the modernization project, modernization theory of the late 1960s continued to characterize tradition and modernity in dichotomous terms. What Randall and Theobald (1985: 65) call "modernization revisionism" was in the end an effort to point to the resilience of tradition and served as a warning to earlier optimists about the possibilities of transforming the Third World.

No author captures the contradictions of modernization revisionism more than Gunnar Myrdal, author of the three-volume *Asian Drama* (1968). In the prologue to this massive work, Myrdal encouraged theorists to move beyond Cold War national security concerns, Western concepts and methodologies, and even sympathy that some Western intellectuals display toward underdeveloped regions (1968: 19–23). According to Myrdal, such concerns need to be replaced with scientific objectivity in order to eliminate all biases:

> It is the ethos of scientific inquiry that truth and blunt truth-speaking are wholesome. . . . Illusions handicap the pursuit of knowledge and they obstruct efforts to make planning for development fully effective and successful. . . . Facts should be stated coldly: understatements, as well as overstatements, represent biases (1968: 23).

Myrdal sought to bring the cold-blooded reason of scientific and technical discourse to bear upon what in his view had been passionate and therefore biased analysis of South Asia.

What are the "facts" at issue? In an apparent break with other theorists of modernization such as Rostow, Myrdal argued that "the basic social and economic structure of the countries is radically different from that existing in advanced Western countries" (1968: 26). However, instead of arguing that this requires an adjustment in Western thinking, Myrdal argued that "the problem of development in South Asia is one calling for induced changes in that social and institutional structure, as it hinders economic development" (1968: 26).

The basic economic and social structure described by Myrdal represents, as it did for modernization theorists, an obstacle to the realization of "modernization ideals" (Myrdal 1968: 57). Modernization ideals include rationality and the eradication of superstitious and illogical reasoning. Planning, the "rationally coordinated system of policy measures that can bring about development," is also required (Myrdal 1968: 58). As a supporter of the liberal welfare state, Myrdal also recommended increased incomes and greater income equality, but he devotes the most space to a discussion of the need to improve institutions and attitudes. Institutionally, modernization requires an "integrated national community," where barriers of "caste, color, religion, ethnic origin, culture, language and provincial loyalties would be broken down" (Myrdal 1968: 60). Attitudinal change implies the "creation of the 'new man,' or the 'modern man,' the

'citizen of the new state,' the 'man in the era of science,' the 'industrial man,' and so forth (1968: 61)."
Myrdal listed the traits associated with modern man is as follows:

- Efficiency
- Diligence
- Orderliness
- Punctuality
- Frugality
- Scrupulous honesty (which pays in the long run and is a
  condition for raising efficiency in all social and economic
  relations)
- Rationality in decisions on action (liberation from reliance on
  static customs, from group allegiances and favoritism, from su-
  perstitious beliefs and prejudices, approaching the rationally
  calculating "economic man" of Western liberal ideology)
- Preparedness for change (for experimentation along new
  lines, and for moving around spatially, economically, socially)
- Alertness for opportunities as they arise in a changing world
- Energetic enterprise
- Integrity and self-reliance
- Cooperativeness (not limiting but redirecting egoistic striving
  in a socially beneficial channel; acceptance of responsibility
  for the welfare of the community and nation)
- Willingness to take the long view (and to forego short-term
  profiteering; subordination of speculation to investment and
  of commerce and finance to production, etc.).

Like Inkeles and Smith, the SSRC committee, and other early
modernization theorists, Myrdal simultaneously objectifies traditional society and associates it with social constructions of femininity.
For Myrdal, modern attitudes and institutions are clearly superior to
traditional ones. These traits cluster along the familiar social constructions of male and female and they serve to denigrate the tradi-
tional/feminine at the expense of the modern/masculine. Like early
modernization theory, underlying Myrdal's construction of tradition
and modernity is a presentation of the "great divide" between the
sexes (Rooney 1991: 92). On the one side is reason, modernity, and
discipline; on the other is irrationality, tradition, and chaos.
Myrdal brings his scientific objectivity to bear on the "anti-rational
attitudes" characteristic of Asian societies and poses the question
bluntly for modernization theorists: "The main practical problem
from the point of view of modernization ideals . . . is whether and

how this complex of emotions can be controlled in the interests of national consolidation, rationalism, planning, and coordination of national policies for development" (Myrdal 1968: 121–122). The chief institution for harnessing these forces should be the state itself, but in Asia it is "soft," primarily because it exists in a socioeconomic environment where there has been little evolution from the "primitive and static village organization" (Myrdal 1968: 897). Nationalism and struggles for independence created the momentum for realizing the modernization ideals, but because nationalist movements failed to transform "stagnant" rural structures, the state lacks the capacity for national planning. Given the continued prevalence of structures of obligations along kinship and family lines, policies developed by the soft state are usually not enforced, and "national governments require extraordinarily little of their citizens" (Myrdal 1968: 896).

Myrdal differs from other modernization theorists largely in his sympathetic (and realistic) recognition of the debilitating effects of colonialism and his praise for efforts on the part of the postcolonial state to implement more egalitarian and redistributive social policies (Myrdal 1968: 896–897). Nevertheless, he portrays tradition as an aspect of "primitive and static village organization" and modernity with a national, integrated state inhabited by "scientific" and "industrial" men who have the capacity to overcome the stagnant village relations of obligation based on kin and familial relations. Like Inkeles and Smith, Myrdal makes implicit but undeniable linkages between becoming modern and social constructions of masculinity. His anxiety about the continued power of tradition and the feminine is evident in his advice to political leaders in Asia:

> In many respects a large and rapid change of attitudes and institutions is not more difficult than a series of small and gradual changes—just as a plunge into cold water is less painful than slow immersion . . . there is less chance for resistance when the change is rapid and multiple (Myrdal 1968: 1910).

Myrdal also employs language and imagery associated with battles and war in his analysis of the challenges to modernization. For example, he notes that resistance to modernization plans should be expected, and thus "attacking on a broad front" is preferable to the "narrow front of investment and production" (Myrdal 1968: 1910). South Asian government leaders are criticized for their lack of determination and unwillingness to apply compulsion in various "campaigns" to enact and enforce laws and regulations. Myrdal even approvingly quotes U.S. jurist Learned Hand to the effect that "law is violence": the use of force for social ends is not a retreat from democracy (Myrdal 1968: 1909). He also agrees with Tibor Mende, another Western observer of Asian politics, who wrote:

> In an inert society where the deformations of the past have accumulated, you are exactly in the same situation as the man who cuts a clearing in the jungle, if you go on attacking one problem; that clearing will not resist the jungle, when it grows back, it will disappear. Either you go at it seriously or better you don't touch it, because you will be disillusioned (quoted in Myrdal 1968: 1907).

The lone male clearing the jungle as a metaphor for attacking deformations of the past is a powerful image that permeates Myrdal's reading of the challenge facing leaders engaged in the struggle for modernization. Twenty years later, scholars in African studies revived Myrdal's analysis of the soft state.

▲ The Soft State in Africa

Goran Hyden (1983a) revived the concept of the soft state and argued that it captured the dynamics of Africa's political economy. In his chronicle of the shifts in the study of Africa from the 1960s to the 1980s, he notes that in the 1960s the major focus was on domestic actors and nationalist politics. Dependency theory was the major focus in the 1970s, but the failures of dependency theory led to a shift back toward domestic politics (Hyden 1987: 117–119). He portrays dependency theory as a mechanistic approach focused solely on external factors, while the shift toward domestic politics represents an attempt to understand the "full dynamics" of development (Hyden 1987: 119). These dynamics cannot be understood through analysis of statistics and the study of formal structures; rather, "hidden processes," the "vibrancy of things African" (Hyden 1990: 247), and the peasant mode of production constitute the underlying material reality of African political economy. Hyden's characterization of the various phases in theorizing about Africa is repeated uncritically by a number of other Africanists (e.g., Shaw 1991; Nyang'oro 1989; Bratton 1989). Only a few authors have claimed that Hyden's work represents an attempt to revive modernization theory of the 1960s. In addition, Hyden relies upon implicit devices used by modernization theorists to anchor tradition and modernity in social constructions of femininity and masculinity.

Hyden's revival of modernization theory began with the publication of *Beyond Ujamaa* in 1980 and has continued, with one major and one minor shift in focus, throughout the 1980s and early 1990s (Hyden 1980; 1983a; 1983b; 1985; 1986; 1987; 1989; 1990; 1992; and

Hyden and Peters, 1991). A number of key concepts and arguments recur in his writings. The first is one that, like Myrdal, he constantly contradicts. On the one hand he argues for the historical specificity of Africa, claiming that comparisons with Europe and Asia, and the derivation of concepts from development in these two regions of the world, are unhelpful. It is interesting that he echoes Myrdal by criticizing attempts to apply Western concepts to African conditions (Hyden 1985: 191). These efforts fail to realize the "material and social realities of the continent." Comparing modernization to the developmental stages of human beings, he argues that Africa was "born into a world characterized by its faith in progress" and has "been brought into adulthood with little respect for its dynamics and abilities" (Hyden 1990: 245; Hyden 1985: 191). Like the modernization theorists of the SSRC, Hyden implies that traditional societies are in a state of helplessness, while modernity represents (male) maturity. On the other hand, he frequently compares Africa with Europe and Asia in order to bolster his own arguments and downplay the significance of external factors. For example, he argues that Barrington Moore's description of the rise of capitalism in Europe also describes Africa, although the process by which the state extracts surplus from peasantry is "still at an incipient stage" (Hyden 1983b: 69). Hyden argues that "the early phases of class formation in industrial society" should be studied in order to gain insight into the requisites for African development (1983a: 22). There are frequent references to the pattern of development of capitalism and state power in Europe and Asia, while at the same time an insistence that Africa is unique (Hyden 1980: 191; 1983b: 399). This crucial maneuver is what allows Hyden to insist that his approach differs from both modernization and dependency theorists. It appears that his argument with modernization theorists is over the nature of the African peasantry. It appears that his argument with dependency theorists is over the influence of imperialism. In fact, despite the use of seemingly different concepts, Hyden reproduces the chief assumption of modernization theory, which is that the pattern of development in the West can be repeated in Africa. The problem is that African leaders and international donors have failed to recognize that Africa is still "backward" (Hyden 1983a: 148). Its economies remain precapitalist; there is no viable bourgeoisie; and attitudes and behavior are largely prescientific (Hyden 1983a: 5, 45). These characteristics make it structurally impossible for development and growth to take place. African leaders, often in collaboration with international donors, have tried to skip stages in development, which is impossible, according to Hyden: there are "no shortcuts" to progress.

For Hyden, the key material reality in Africa is the absence of a feudal tradition (Hyden 1985: 191; 1986: 55). Because long-distance trade was the key to the accumulation of surplus and there was little if any shortage of land, the mode of production remains largely pre-capitalist. Thus it appears that Hyden, unlike modernization theo-rists, is presenting traditional society as a reflection of material con-ditions rather than cultural "backwardness." He misleadingly claims that his approach is a materialist and orthodox Marxist one (Hyden 1983a: xiv, 4, 191).

For Hyden then, tradition has its basis in the peasant mode of production, which operates according to its own logic, interestingly defined as the "economy of affection," a cultural and social system that reflects prevailing technology and patterns of land ownership in the African countryside. He derives the term from Chayanov, who ar-gued that nonmarket aspects of production and consumption are val-ued more than maximizing monetary values (Hyden 1987: 120). The economy of affection constitutes an alternative economy, one that "lacks regular cost-benefit considerations associated with economic action under either capitalism or socialism" (Hyden 1983b: 71). In-stead of the development of the means of production, the "needs of man" take precedence (Hyden 1980: 14). Peasants and workers "do not place personal economic achievement above family solidarity" (Hyden 1980: 161).

Despite Hyden's purportedly materialistic explanation of the economy of affection, both it and the peasant mode of production serve as referents to traditional society as conceived by moderniza-tion theorists. It has distinct gender dimensions as well. The econ-omy of affection is "guided by the principles of reciprocity embed-ded in customary rules rather than universal and abstract laws from above" (Hyden 1987: 117–118). These precapitalist social formations are repeatedly characterized by their parochialism and particularism (Hyden 1989: 6; 1987: 121). The economy of affection is portrayed as fragmented and centrifugal, and operating on the basis of its "own social logic" that is immune to state power (Hyden 1983a: 11). It is "by definition hostile to bureaucratic principles common to Western societies" (Hyden 1986: 61). These societies are also capable of re-sisting modern ways of life embodied in the city:

> The very complexity of life in the city reinforces punctuality, calcu-lability, and exactness and leads to a matter of fact attitude in deal-ing with men and things. . . . The urban man is an intellectual nomad, quite homeless, a microcosm. World history is city history (Hyden 1985: 201).

In placing the economy of affection outside of world history Hyden manages to juxtapose, as modernization theorists did, the rational, the urban, and the modern, with the parochial, the rural, the tradi-tional. These oppositions also present powerful gender stereotypes.

Women stand at the center of the economy of affection, the traditional economy; they embody tradition and provincialism. To be modern is to transcend those traits associated with the feminized economy of affection. The mode of social organization that characterizes the economy of affection are qualities that historically have been linked with the home: community, reciprocity, and solidarity, rather than the market, exchange, and self-interest (Hyden 1990: 250).

Hyden goes beyond modernization theorists and Myrdal in his arguments about the extent to which the economy of affection is no longer confined to the rural areas. The "precapitalist values embodied in rural society tend to permeate social behavior and interactions in the towns" (Hyden 1985: 207; see also 1987: 121). The state itself is regarded as an arena for enhancing kinship and familial relations, the cornerstone of the economy of affection (Hyden 1986: 61). The state, according to Hyden, lacks structural roots in society; it is an artifact of colonial rule and has no effective means of extracting surplus from the peasantry. In fact, principles of state governance are guided by the dictates of the economy of affection, thus making the state "soft," a personalized, particularistic, and patrimonial institution (Hyden 1989: 5–6).

Hyden's preoccupation is with making the soft state "hard," or "firmer and more resolute" (Hyden 1983b: 198). In revealing imagery he describes the hardened state as one that has broken the backbone of the economy of affection (Hyden 1986: 70). The only forces capable of carrying out this "painful function" are "businessmen and manufacturers who from a city base can articulate their demands for policies that enhance productivity or efficiency" among the peasantry (Hyden 1986: 71). In a classic restatement of the modernization formulation, Hyden calls for placing the bourgeoisie in the "driver's seat," with cities serving as the "powerful engine" of development (Hyden 1986: 71). Hyden also compares the incipient bourgeoisie in Africa to Prometheus. Like struggling Prometheus, the emerging bourgeoisie in Africa is locked in battle with the economy of affection and can only be free with a transformation that brings capital and labor into conflict: "Prometheus's emancipation and thus his ability to perform for Africa the same historical role he has done in other modernizing societies" is the key to achieving state hardness (Hyden 1985: 212).

▲ Uncaptured Peasants and the Soft State

In *Beyond Ujamaa* (1980) Hyden presents his thesis about the structural anomaly of the rural peasantry in Africa and a case study of

Tanzania. He discusses both German and British colonial policies with regard to the peasantry, the policies of the early independence government under Julius Nyerere's leadership, and the policy of *ujamaa*, a word in Swahili that means familyhood and that was a cornerstone of Nyerere's vision of African socialism. The concept was officially adopted by the Tanganyika African National Union (TANU), the ruling party, in Arusha in 1967. The Arusha Declaration set in motion a whole series of programs. Hyden focuses most of his discussion on the campaign to create communal villages, which was speeded up in 1973 with a policy called "villagization" that included coercion against peasants who resisted moving from their villages. He also discusses *Mwongozo,* the party guidelines issued in 1971 that attempted to replace one-person management with socialist and participatory worker's control in state-owned enterprises (also called parastatals). *No Shortcuts* (1983a) is more general and uses examples from a number of sub-Saharan African countries to make a case for capitalism, voluntary organizations, and revised lending practices by international donors.

In *Beyond Ujamaa*, Hyden provides a sympathetic account of peasant reaction to the imposition of German and British colonial rule in Tanzania. He notes that colonial perceptions about idle peasants were in fact a product of the unreasonable demands placed on peasants who sought both to produce for colonial markets and at the same time to meet household needs (Hyden 1980: 46). Hyden's thesis, however, is that German and British colonialism did not do enough to ensure the development of capitalist relations of production. Capitalist penetration "destroyed precolonial modes of production but it did not pave the way for capitalism" (Hyden 1980: 42). Peasant rebellions in colonial Tanzania are explained as peasant reaction to encroachment upon the household, "the fulcrum of peasant autonomy" (Hyden 1980: 64). The nationalist movement that emerged in the 1950s represented a coalition led by petit-bourgeois leaders who had "not totally defected from the economy of affection" (Hyden 1980: 65) and a peasantry that remained firmly ensconced in the economy of affection. The persistence of precapitalist relations, along with a nationalist leadership with one foot in the economy of affection and the other in the public realm, explain the failures of postindependence policies. As Hyden (1980: 219) puts it: "Small is powerful and as such constitutes an obstacle to development."

The economy of affection in postindependence Tanzania resembles a mysterious bog where programs are announced but rarely implemented. Peasants were capable of convincing frustrated government officials that they supported projects toward which, in fact, they were indifferent (Hyden 1980: 87). Peasant villages continued to frustrate the implementation of government policies as government officials adopted the economy of affection. Candidates in TANU-controlled elections who devoted too much effort to government and party work and not enough to the locality were voted out of office (Hyden 1980: 89). *Ujamaa*, the policy launched with the Arusha Declaration, ended up placing government and party officials in the "trap of the economy of affection" (Hyden 1980: 109).

The Arusha Declaration nationalized property, instituted a leadership code for party leaders, and announced that communal villages would be created in the rural areas. Hyden presents it as a contradictory policy in that, on the one hand, President Nyerere attempted to formulate the principles of the economy of affection—respect, common property, and an obligation to work—"into a national strategy of development" (Hyden 1980: 98) while, on the other hand, it represented an attempt to "round up" the party leadership and force them to shift their loyalties from the economy of affection to the state (Hyden 1980: 97). According to Hyden, the policy was bound to fail because only the peasant household can provide the basis of the economy of affection. Thus peasants responded selectively to government exhortations to increase productivity and resisted efforts to disturb the economy of affection.

After three years of resistance on the part of peasant communities, President Nyerere and the party imposed the forced "villagization" policy to rid peasant communities once and for all of their autonomy and ability to exercise the "exit" option in the face of market encroachment. Forcing village settlements was only a partial success because of the strength of the economy of affection, which continued to influence the behavior of government officials and encouraged corruption. In Hyden's words, "there was an extension of the economy of affection into the party organization," an unintended consequence of party efforts to saturate the countryside with its representatives (Hyden 1980: 110). In this sense, villagization represented the clash between the forces of tradition and modernity, and the forces of tradition prevailed.

In fact, government officials charged with carrying out compulsory village settlements castigated peasants as negative, superstitious, and backward, an excellent example of the extent to which definitions of development and modernization are shared by state leaders in Africa and outside donors. After 1973, when Nyerere announced compulsory "villagization," the government sought to reduce the power of wealthier farmers in the rural areas and government reorganization was carried out in order to make local government more responsive to the peasantry (Hyden 1980: 130–135). Hyden describes these efforts as an attempt to replace the capitalist market with a political marketplace (Hyden 1980: 134; 138; 154). He characterizes it as the replacement of "an essentially capitalist-inspired superstructure with an institutional formation that more directly reflects the pre-capitalist relations of the country" (Hyden 1980: 139).

Hyden also discusses the "pre-capitalist takeover" of the public sector after the publication of *Mwongozo* in 1971. Before that, the state sector is portrayed by Hyden as a capitalist enclave. *Mwongozo* established party militias in parastatals (the state-owned sector) to combat capitalist practices. According to Hyden, this innovation was the beginning of the end of the strict discipline imposed by modern capitalist structures. Employees began to relate to each other as human beings rather than "cogs in a wheel" (Hyden 1980: 163). Managers lost their ability to discipline workers as peasants and increasingly viewed *Mwongozo* as an opportunity to enrich themselves and the economy of affection at the expense of the state sector.

Lemarchand (1989: 40–41) argues that Hyden rejects the notion that such peasant reactions could be rational, but in fact Hyden points repeatedly to the inherent logic and rationality of the economy of affection (see, for example, Hyden 1980: 118, 140, 165). The crucial issue is the comparison that Hyden makes between the logic of the economy of affection and the logic of the modern state: the former is partial, fragmented, and buried within familial and clan-based particularisms. The latter is the universal, integrationist, and developmentalist state. The conflict is one between "peasant rationality, as determined by the production structures in the villages, and government rationality as determined by macro-economic demands" (Hyden 1980: 149). The references to similar social constructions of gender differences are unmistakable. Peasant rationality in the rural areas is associated with historically female-centered work: nurturance, reciprocity, and family life. Hyden also calls forth a historical strand of Western political thought that has portrayed the feminine as powerful, inscrutable, and dangerous. As Tanzanian bureaucrats pursue the peasantry enmeshed within the economy of affection, they attempt to capture them, but they are incapable of mastery over or even manipulation of this moral economy. In fact, they risk being swallowed up within it. He describes shrewd peasant behavior in response to village visits by government officials:

> Thus the peasants soon learned ways of inducing the officials to believe that they were enjoying widespread support. Most important was to appear for political meetings and generally applaud and support the development ethic of the officials (1980: 87).

This characterization resonates with the ambivalence that Jordanova (1980: 49) found in the writings of eighteenth-century Enlightenment thinkers: "Women are tougher and softer, more vulnerable and tenacious of life than men." Hyden also depicts the female-centered economy of affection as soft but resilient, living a precarious existence but nevertheless capable of challenging the state.

Hyden was much more sanguine about the possibilities for socialist transformation in 1980. He recommended breaking the strength of the economy of affection and encouraging the articulation of class conflicts in order to lay the groundwork for socialist relations of production. In other words, he saw merit in the strategy of creating the preconditions for socialism and argued that, putatively, socialist regimes were more likely to provide a hospitable environment for the realization of state power vis-à-vis the economy of affection (Hyden 1980: 197). By 1983, Hyden made strenuous arguments for the superiority of capitalism rather than socialism. The development of a modernization framework, with its gendered foundations, became more prominent and insistent as well.

In *No Shortcuts* (1983a) Hyden is even more impressed with the tenacity of the economy of affection in Africa and the ability of the peasants to escape state-imposed regulations. The state itself begins to take on the characteristics of the female-centered household: it has been "swamped" by the economy of affection. Hyden argues that the leaders of the postcolonial state have completely caved in to the logic of the peasant mode of production, primarily because they have understandably sought to reconstruct the character of the postcolonial state itself: from authoritarian to democratic, hierarchical to popular, and centralized to participatory (Hyden 1983a: 19). However, in doing so they have sacrificed the orderliness of the public realm for the chaos of the household. In fact, the state itself has become an arena where reciprocity, support networks, and their negative counterparts of nepotism, corruption, and patronage are fully realized. The state, in other words, has come to resemble the female-headed household and is incapable of carrying out efficient development. The realization of the economy of affection in state structures has resulted in chaos and disorder. The task for domestic and international planners is to clean up the mess and reinstitute proper (masculine) modes of interaction.

Hyden (1983a: 11) does note that the economy of affection has played an important role in basic survival, social maintenance, and development. However, he also depicts the economy of affection as a "springboard" for the development of the instrumental and rational attitudes necessary for modernity and development. In general, the economy of affection "holds back development by delaying changes in behavioral institutions capable of sustaining economic growth at the national level" (Hyden 1983a: 17). This juxtaposition of the

positive and negative aspects of the economy of affection is important for Hyden's arguments later in the text of *No Shortcuts,* when he
proposes that international donors must bypass the state in their efforts to aid entrepreneurs and laborers "who wish to cut their ties
with the economy of affection but who very often find it difficult to
do so because there is not enough recognition of their needs by the
formal structures of the economy" (Hyden 1983a: 154). In fact, in remarkably masculinist terms, Hyden discusses these individuals as
"springing out" of the economy of affection (Hyden 1983a: 155). In
provocative language, Hyden suggests that after these entrepreneurs
have sprung from the economy of affection, they should be further
"weaned" by international donors. This extensive international involvement is necessary because African nationalists, in rejecting capitalism in the early years of independence, performed a "historical
abortion" because they blocked the birth of a local bourgeoisie
(Hyden 1983a: 200). Strengthening these individuals will allow them
to "get closer to the market and its challenges" (Hyden 1983a: 156).
Di Stefano (1991a: 83–85) has noted how a key feature of modern
thought has been its insistence that humans are "thoroughly atomistic," which affirms the "self-sufficiency of man alone in the midst of
other men." Hyden's portrayal of the positive aspects of the economy
of affection—nurturance, reciprocity, and survival—also carries po-
tent constructions of female mystery and power which men must
"spring from" in order to achieve modernity.

A number of other important and implicitly gendered themes
emerge in *No Shortcuts.* First, Hyden makes a call for the severance
of attachment to precapitalist roots on the part of African leaders
(1983a; 50–51). In essence, Hyden is calling on African leaders to be
men of the market through the "institutionalization of impersonal
calculative principles" (1983a: 51). Severing all ties with the economy of affection is necessary for modernity. Ekeh (1975: 106) has
highlighted the difficulties of breaking ties with what he terms the
"primordial" public realm. The gains are not material but "intangi-
ble, immaterial benefits in the form of identity or psychological security." As Hirschmann (1989: 1230) puts it, "Becoming male entails
making a radical break with primary femininity, represented by the
mother, resulting from an overemphasis upon separation; a boy defines himself against the mother, as not-mother." There is an anxious plea to Hyden's tone that reflects a concern with more than the
market. Revulsion toward the economy of affection and the female-
centered household also frames Hyden's championing of markets,
profits, and impersonal calculations of efficiency. Hyden (1983a: 23)
describes the role of entrepreneurs in heroic terms, as "architects of
the complex superstructure that we associate with modern industrial

society," and chides Africans for being superstitious of entrepre-
neurialism:

> Africa needs those men of destiny who can throw off the bonds im-
> posed by the economy of affection and through their actions . . .
> produce a more effective base for the pursuit of necessary macro-
> economic functions in society (1983a: 24).

Second, Hyden argues that, despite the power of the privatized
household, African leaders do have a vision of politics that is similar
to that which has informed the vision of Western thinkers from
Hobbes to Marx. Hyden labels it the "blueprint" approach, a pen-
chant for full-blown plans based on rational principles of planning
(1983a: 63–64). The blueprint approach serves as a counterweight to
the centrifugal pressures that originate in the economy of affection.
Blueprints also hold out the promise of a brighter future and provide a bridge between foreign donors and state planners. It is interesting to note that Hyden praises these visions of rational planning
but argues that they are not realistic in the face of a situation in
which African farmers control resources.

Third, Hyden makes a strenuous plea for capitalism, thus coming
full circle and adopting an uncritical Parsonian endorsement of the
benefits of liberal democratic capitalism. The economy of affection
"can be transcended only by a bourgeois class which from positions
outside government can demand its services in a reliable and efficient manner" (1983a: 78). The relations among people have to be
organized around the market in order to ensure development
(1983a: 182). As long as the economy of affection prevails, rudimentary technology and a culture that resists scientific innovation and
entrepreneurial talent will thwart Africa's efforts to enlarge the
arena of politics (1983b: 79). In Hyden's scenario, the self-regulating
and calculating bourgeoisie (businessmen and manufacturers) con-
fronts the unproductive female-headed household.

Furthermore, bourgeois man must be aided by international
donors: "The international donors can become effective in assisting
African governments only once there are macro-economic institutions and a firm state in place and at work" (Hyden 1983a: 168).
Thus far donor agencies have been willing to assist soft states and in
fact have ensured their survival, although the operations of these
donors in Africa should be likened to private firms seeking "greater
control over a difficult task environment" (Hyden 1983a: 178).
Hyden argues that small and medium-sized businesses in Africa
should be the recipients of aid, and that initially the state should be
bypassed as much as possible. The key problem is that the economy

of affection "keeps African society as a whole at a much higher temperature," thus international funding should "make it increasingly possible for the local entrepreneur to leave the comfortable temperature of the economy of affection without being left in the cold" (Hyden 1983a: 186). As these African businesses begin to flourish, they can provide the necessary pressure on the soft state and create a disciplined government. The state will become an instrument of bourgeois men rather than a reflection of the values represented in the theory by peasant women.

In sum, the takeover of the state by the economy of affection evokes images of engulfment. Despite an understandable longing for the nurturance and sustenance provided by the economy of affection, African leaders must achieve autonomy and separation from the household. This break can be accomplished only by the emergence of bourgeois man, or rational economic man, assisted by international donors. The ability of African leaders to imagine a public world where the economy of affection is tamed reinforces the underlying theme of Hyden's and modernization theory's work as well: African leaders are like "us" and share similar conceptions of an idealized public realm inhabited by self-sufficient and autonomous men. Development for Hyden is a polarized battleground between the primordial (m)other and the civilized state.

▲ Development as a Battle (Between the Sexes)

It has been shown how Hyden shares with modernization theorists a view of development that is evolutionary, in which African societies begin from "backwardness" and "catch up" with the West (with no shortcuts allowed). Hyden also uses powerful metaphors that treat development as a battle, struggle, or war. In *Beyond Ujamaa* (1980: 125), he argues that the major failure of villagization in Tanzania was failure to "get at" the peasantry. The challenge facing both socialist and capitalist regimes is one of "penetrating" precapitalist modes of production, where the labor force is "held captive" in precapitalist bonds of affection (Hyden 1980: 160). He refers to policy areas as "fronts" where the peasant mode must be "conquered" in order to achieve development (Hyden 1980: 167, 108). The peasantry itself is a "target group" of governmental efforts to achieve control over the economy of affection. In fact, capitalism itself is depicted as, among other things, "a general sense of control of the forces of nature" (Hyden 1980: 200).

In *No Shortcuts*, Hyden depicts the peasantry and the economy of affection as engaged in a silent guerrilla struggle "aimed at bringing a system down" (1983a: 21). He writes (1983a: 161) with alarm about the "invasion of clan politics" into the state arena and argues (1983a: 91) that the chief goal of the state should be to "contain" those forces. In fact, he describes the major battle facing Africa as a "battle between forces defending those precapitalist formations and those— still much weaker—trying to conquer them" (1983a: 193). State leaders are described as being held to "ransom by their own uncaptured peasantry" (1983a: 188). In one especially vivid passage (1983a: 148), he compares developmental progress with rape:

> Africa is still struggling to build indigenous sources of economic growth when most of its economies have barely progressed beyond "rape" of their hinterlands and mineral wealth for export. Assuming that the modern state is worth striving for, it is not difficult to see that in these senses Africa is in a unique historical situation where it is truly "backward."

In sum, the abstract masculinity described by object relations theory is interwoven in Hyden's account of the key dilemmas faced by African leaders, businessmen, and farmers in their efforts to resolve the desires for fusion with and independence from the economy of affection. In *No Shortcuts,* Hyden's language becomes particularly charged: the economy of affection is described as a place of warmth and men are encouraged to spring from it and establish an identity in opposition to this powerful community. The economy of affection is also in a sense held responsible for what has gone wrong with Africa's development. Affective relations have permeated and invaded the state and threaten total engulfment. Hyden's call for a flight from community expresses "the adult and detectably modern masculine desire for self-generation and a species generation that can be self-consciously willed, created, and controlled" (Di Stefano 1991a: 49–50). Hyden approvingly notes that modernity signifies that the individual is no longer at the mercy of such highly charged relationships but is rather "engulfed by the *nature artificielle,* a captive of the system, or perhaps more appropriately, a cog in a wheel" (1983a: 39).

Hyden's conception of private and public is also a familiar rendering of the gendered symbolism historically associated with the two realms. He agrees with Peter Ekeh that in Africa there are two public realms rather than one, as in the West. Ekeh (1975: 91) defines politics as the "activities of individuals insofar as they impinge on the public realm made up of the collective interests of the citizenry." What the individual does in "his own home," on the other hand, is considered a private matter. Ekeh (1975: 92) defines the two publics in Africa as a primordial public realm, which "operates on the same imperatives as the private realm," and the civic public, which is

composed of the inherited formal structures of colonial rule (the bureaucracy, civil service, police, and so forth). According to Ekeh
(1975: 106), the lack of legitimacy of the civic public structures
means that the leadership continues to have duties and moral obligations to the primordial public realm. In language that parallels psychological accounts of the moral and contextual reasoning of
women, Ekeh (1975: 106, 108) describes the relationship of African
leaders to the primordial public as a moral one: "The individual sees
his duties as moral obligations to benefit and sustain a primordial
public of which he is a member. The primordial public is a source of
identity and security. . . . Like most moral spheres, the relationship
between the individual and his primordial public cannot be exhausted by economic equations. There is more to all moral duties
than the material worth of the duties themselves." Ekeh presents an
important contrast between moral obligation (primordial) and
rights and duties based on calculation and instrumental reasoning
(civic). According to both Hyden (1983a: 39) and Ekeh (1975: 108),
only the disappearance of the primordial public realm can ensure
the rationalization of public life. Public life must thus be limited to
the self-sufficient transactions of rational men. Ironically, Hyden's
negative characterization of the African state suspended in midair
returns in his formulation of the civic public realm. He believes that
African leaders need to construct a public space that is apart from
and stands over and above the affective relations of the private
realm. Hyden's stark vision is ultimately an exclusionary and masculinist defense against the "messy" passions, obligations, and moral-
ity of the household.

▲ Successor Theories of the Soft State

Recycled modernization theory with its gendered categories can be
found in the work of other Africanists who have embraced the soft-
state paradigm. Rothchild (1985: 2), for example, plaintively asks,
"How can the soft be hardened?" The African state has achieved only
partial autonomy because of its limited ability to distance itself from
society. Competence, effectiveness, capacity, ability, management
skills, discipline, coercive power, and control are presented as the
goals that African leaders should embrace, traits which also characterize contemporary constructions of masculinity. African leaders are
conceived of as solitary subjects doing battle with social forces that
threaten to engulf them. It is interesting to note the extent to which
patron-client relations, clan and kinship ties, and other "traditional"
forms of social exchange are treated as impediments to modernity.

Such relationships are based upon interconnectedness, interrelatedness, dependence, and reciprocity, all of which present challenges to African leaders in their efforts to conduct government business in an unencumbered manner.

In his vividly entitled article, "The Quest for State 'Hardness' in Africa," Forrest (1988) reiterates Hyden's suggestive treatment of hard and soft states and offers the following sexualized imagery of state hardness:

> (1) structural autonomy, whereby state institutions, leaders, and officials effectively remove themselves from the influence of societal actors . . . and make decisions independently of social forces, (2) the political penetration of society, by which national leaders and governmental institutions secure clear-cut hegemony . . . (3) the extraction of resources from the most productive sectors of society, (4) ideological legitimation . . . official doctrines to defend and justify the achievement of autonomy, penetration, and extraction (1988: 423).

The struggle for mastery and autonomy over "social forces" is, as Di Stefano puts it, an "ultraconflictual" account of social relations that has gendered connotations (Di Stefano 1991a: 23). The anthropomorphized state undertakes vigorous efforts to deny dependence, relations, needs, and other socially constructed feminine attributes (Chodorow 1989: 109–110). The unquestioned and assumed function of the state is to "establish aims and interests which differ from and often are opposed to those of individuals and groups within society" (Forrest 1988: 424). These groups and individuals are usually "traditional" actors such as chiefs, clan, and ethnic leaders (Forrest 1988: 426). Depictions of state leaders engaged in hostile combat with dangerous forces of tradition helps demonstrate that Hyden's view is not anomalous but rather reflects a distinctive approach in understanding challenges to development.

Nyang'oro (1989: 116) also characterizes peasant society as "essentially self-limiting, backward, and operating in a framework and logic that limits the expansion of productive forces." Like Callaghy, he portrays the state-society struggle in ultracompetitive terms, as the "state attempting to assert its control over the population while the population struggles to retain its autonomous existence" (Nyang'oro 1989: 131). He psychologizes the problems faced by African leaders by arguing that they are "confused" and need to acknowledge "misplaced development priorities, essential incompetence, and ultimately the question of legitimacy" (Nyang'oro 1989: 147, 146).

> There must evolve in Africa a corps of leaders who are dedicated to change and a genuinely progressive and developmental ideology,

who must deliberately work to eradicate the particularistic and parochial mentality so ingrained in the present leadership (Nyang'oro 1989: 148).

Claude Ake (1985: 6), who earlier took a more radical approach to African political economy, has come to share this perspective on the essential problem facing contemporary Africa. For Ake, the peasantry in Africa exists outside of civil society, "enmeshed in a web of social relations characterized by what can only be described, following Durkheim, as mechanical solidarity" (Ake 1985: 9). In an interesting characterization, Ake (1985: 10) labels the politics of postindependence Nigeria as the "politics of anxiety" because of the indiscipline and anarchy that retard the development of "capitalist rationality" (1985: 17). Like Hyden, Jackson and Rosberg, Callaghy, and Nyang'oro, Ake portrays the state in terms that have been used to describe traditional societies and women as well. State practices are "precapitalist" and plagued by inefficiency and corruption rather than showing "formal freedom, equality, and universalism" (1985: 15).

▲ Patrimonial States

Callaghy's (1984: xi) work on the Zairean state differs from Hyden's in that he accepts many of the dependency theory positions regarding the importance of imperialism; and he argues against dualisms by noting that the African state contains a mix of traditional and modern attributes:

> Like their early modern European predecessors, most African states today are centralizing, but distinctively limited, authoritarian patrimonial-bureaucratic states. They have low levels of development and penetration and limited coercive and implementation capabilities. Politics is highly personalized, and a ruling class is emerging, with the gap between the rulers and the ruled increasing (1984: 59).

As an early modern state, Zaire (like other African countries) has "made some progress toward acquiring the characteristics of a modern state" but still has "substantial distance to travel before becoming predominately modern" (1984: 14). Callaghy thus lauds the characteristics of the modern state that require increasing autonomy, control, separation, and penetration. Although he explicitly argues that the state-society struggle in Zaire should not be viewed as a battle between modernity and tradition, he does argue that struggle defines relations between central authority and "a complex interplay of various particularisms" (1984: 62). Squabbling local chiefdoms, local factions, political entrepreneurs, and patron-client ties all play prominently in Callaghy's script of the state-society struggle. There is no critical analysis of whether the emasculation of these local forces should be inevitable in the march toward modernity. Like modernization theorists, revisionists, and Hyden, he portrays elements of local society locked in struggle with centralizing state practices that are implicitly accepted as inevitable and appropriate. Although Callaghy recognizes that state formation often entails cooptation, the formation of coalitions with local powers, and "contracting" (i.e., the "negotiation of an agreement for the exchange of performance in the future"), he describes the establishment of state power as a "competitive struggle" (1984: 96). It is a fundamentally masculinist view of the nature of development to define it as "the will to dominate" (Callaghy 1984: 82). In interesting language that echoes Hyden, Callaghy employs the jargon of organizational theory to explain the "difficult task environment" faced by African leaders who seek to extend and consolidate state power (Callaghy 1984: 92; See also Hyden 1983b: 178). Faced with "constraints, contingencies, and general uncertainty" from groups in society, the state seeks "compliance, rationality, and certainty" (Callaghy 1984: 90).

Jackson and Rosberg (1982: 5) follow Callaghy and place African governments outside of contemporary history as a "species of early modern states" where "personal ties and dependencies" rather than "public rules and institutions" define political life (Jackson and Rosberg 1982: 1). While Jackson and Rosberg emphasize the authoritarian character of the state and would thus disagree with Hyden's characterization of the state as "soft" and ineffectual, they repeat many of the themes of modernization and soft-state theory. Like Huntington, they present a Hobbesian view of governance in Africa. African politics resembles the state of nature: "The state is a government of men and not laws" (Jackson and Rosberg 1982: 10). Even the African military has been penetrated and "impregnated" by "African sociocultural norms" and thus lacks the unity, professionalism, and esprit de corps that a disciplined military would bring to governance (1982: 33–34). Jackson and Rosberg use repeated juxtapositions to link personal rule with traditional politics as defined by modernization theory. For example, they contrast the discipline and obedience of rational politics with familial or personal loyalty; organizational and social rationality with personal or factional interactions; and public rules and institutions with personal ties (1982: 1, 18–19, 36). Like the SSRC committee, they imply that African governments are in a state of "arrested development," somewhere between "'civil society' and the 'state of nature'" (1982: 40) and that the "responsibility for failing to establish stable regimes . . . rests with political men" (1982: 76).

Jackson and Rosberg also frame politics in this transitional state between the state of nature and civil society as a wrestling match, fight, contest, game, and struggle (1982: 1, 14, 19–20, 48). This is indeed a Hobbesian position: the power of every man is opposed to the other and relationships in society are incessant competitive struggles of "each power over the other" (Macpherson 1962: 22). The appeal of institutionalized government is for instrumental purposes and conflict management. Rules of governance "arise more out of a recognition of their political advantages and uses [rather] than their intrinsic virtues as ideal standards of conduct" (Jackson and Rosberg 1982: 286). Modernity promises a civic polity where politics no longer resembles the messy world of personal connections, family, and clan.

While the terms *state-society struggle* and *personal rule* present a patrimonial definition of the state, thus recognizing that state leaders have independent interests and are capable of arbitrary and capricious behavior, patrimonial frameworks share similar assumptions with modernization and soft-state theorists in the distinction between modern (instrumental) and traditional (personal) politics and a reification of the predictable and rational rules of governance that promise autonomy from the forces that threaten the political order. A state where men play by the rules of the game promises self-reliance. These recurring themes demonstrate a concern with order that in turn rests on a series of dichotomies that portray the dangers of tradition, the economy of affection, and the institutionless polity, on the one hand, with the rational state and ordered polity, on the other, in a way that links them with well-entrenched social constructions of gender differences and perhaps help explain their power and appeal.

▲ Conclusion

Soft-state theory and theories of the "institutionless" African state have usually been seen as reactions against theories of dependency and efforts to categorize African regimes on the basis of ideological self-descriptions. It also reflects a search for the "essence" of domestic political dynamics in Africa in the face of growing marginalization in the world political economy.

A closer examination of the revival of soft-state theory, however, demonstrates that it shares views of tradition and modernity espoused by theorists in the 1950s and 1960s. Tradition is distanced from modernity, for example, and serves as a means for celebrating characteristics of an idealized, modern, rational, public, and masculine world. Mamdani (1985: 190) incisively presents Hyden's argument:

> The real struggle in Africa is that between the forces of capitalism (read: modernity) and those of pre-capitalism (read: tradition). All major problems of contemporary Africa are rooted in its "inherent" pre-capitalist (i.e., traditional) past. . . . The solution is to move from pre-capitalism to capitalism.

The argument in this chapter has been that social constructions of gender differences also permeate the analysis of "soft states" in Asia and Africa. The negative portrayals of tradition are strengthened by the implicit linkages made between tradition and the social constructions of women and feminine attributes. Tradition connotes negative characteristics such as provincialism, inefficiency, superstition, obscurantism—the antithesis of the main traits of constructed male citizenship. Even when the persistence of tradition is recognized as a key factor in the survival of some societies, the practices that define traditional community life, such as reciprocity, kinship, and other communal relationships, are defined as counterproductive. The power of tradition is recognized in sympathetic accounts of attempts by entrepreneurs (rational economic men) to sever dependence upon such ties. Like the SSRC committee, soft-state theorists tend to psychologize efforts to break away from traditional, feminized communities. Hyden even depicts the economy of affection as a warm place from which no man would want to leave—unless guaranteed an opportunity to take on a heroic challenge as architect of a new public order independent of "primordial" ties. Most recently, Hyden (1992: 20) describes development itself as a process whereby "political actors within a given society are able to resolve moral ambiguities and contradictions" about their attachments to the economy of affection. As Sangmpam (1993: 89) notes, "There is a perfect identity of views between the soft state paradigm and modernization theory. The paradigm is a *neo* version of modernization theory."

The lure and power of tradition are further recognized by soft-state theorists in their use of metaphors about battles, struggles, and wars in the effort to develop society. Like the themes emphasized by modernization theorists, societies are characterized as struggling toward a higher order of rationality and efficiency. For Parsons, these societies emerged from primitiveness; soft-state theorists use the more sanitized language of tradition, particularisms, clan politics, and ethnic struggles.

It is significant that struggle and war are the central metaphors in Hyden's narrative of the soft state and are used in the narratives of other theorists as well. This is an intriguing and often disturbing rendering of the classic "battle of the sexes." Hyden describes civic structures as *man-made* accomplishments; they represent a triumph of heroic male leadership that engages in battle with the "silent" peasantry. The struggle is one filled with ambiguity because the economy of affection provides security and comfort even as it thwarts the emergence of self-sufficient and modern men. The ambiguities accompanying independence in Pye's (1971b) formulation of the identity crisis reappear in Hyden's psychological account of leaders with one foot in the economy of affection, and Ekeh's (1975) description of the "psychic turbulence" that new leaders experience in the transition from traditional to modern ways of life. The integuments of the economy of affection constitute a powerful pull on emergent modern men, so much so that the state itself has become a stereotypical woman, incapable even of sustained authoritarianism and steeped in personalism (Hyden 1983a: 45).

Samatar and Samatar (1987: 673) insightfully suggest that the absence of successful revolutionary challenges to world capitalism in the periphery has meant that "modernization theory, as an expression of the general interest of the commanding global and regional classes, was bound to make an appearance." The fall of state communism in the Eastern bloc has intensified the focus on markets and promoting political arrangements to facilitate capitalist development. International donors, as Doornbos (1990: 187) explains, have embraced theoretical criticisms of the state:

> In an age of structural adjustment, liberalization, and privatization, the international community has undergone a major reversal in its appreciation of the role of the African state. . . . Formerly the exclusive recipient, partner, and rationale of international aid and attention, the African state's "most favored" status appears today to have been eclipsed in the eyes of donors by a veil of assumed obsolescence.

In the next chapter I will suggest that theories about the soft, ineffectual, and patrimonial state coincide with the emphasis given by major lenders in Africa to markets, a minimalist state, and a focus on the domestic rather than international determinants of the contemporary crisis in Africa. While many commentators have linked the work of the International Monetary Fund and the World Bank with the current restructuring of the global capitalist economy, there have been no sustained efforts to demonstrate that the formulations of modernization theory, soft-state theory, and related approaches serve as powerful support to policies that emanate from these two bodies and that these policies are also fundamentally gendered around distinctions between public and private—and a worldview

that conceives of entrepreneurship as masculinist activity . Object relations theory and battle metaphors are less helpful in analyzing the
strategic documents of the World Bank: the analysis in the next chapter therefore does not try to replace already existing criticism but
supplements it with a new, feminist angle of vision that shows the relationship between the theory and practice of capitalist development.

▲ 4
Gender and the World Bank: Modernization Theory in Practice

The advice provided by Goran Hyden to the World Bank staff who prepared the analysis of the crisis facing African economies in the late 1980s reflects the influence of the arguments put forward by Hyden and other Africanists on the "softness" of the African state and the necessity of scaling back the public sector and relying on the market to "transform African economies and make them competitive in an increasingly competitive world" (World Bank 1989: xi). The World Bank in effect appropriated the theory of the African soft state in its late 1980s report. The Bank emphasized the soft state's ineffectiveness in bringing about development—on the one hand because of general ineffectual state practices, and on the other because of soft state's role in stifling individual entrepreneurship. This is a seemingly contradictory position: how can an ineffectual state also be credited with stifling entrepreneurial initiative? The Bank implies that the state has become the chief employer—it is overextended, corrupt, and, as chief employer, thwarts any efforts to increase wealth outside of the state. Scaling back the state and replacing it with a minimalist structure will establish the conditions for the emergence of rational economic man and capitalist development.

▲ Overview of Structural Adjustment

The term *structural adjustment* refers to efforts by both the International Monetary Fund (IMF) and the International Bank for Reconstruction and Development (IBRD, or World Bank) to condition further lending to Third World governments on a series of reforms, often drastic and radical, to increase economic growth and ameliorate balance-of-payments difficulties (Anyaoku 1989: 12). The IMF has had stabilization programs in operation for a number of years. The World Bank initiated policy-related lending through structural

69

adjustment loans (SALs) in 1980. SALs are also tied to specified policy reforms such as currency devaluations and the reduction of government subsidies (Paarlberg and Lipton 1991: 484–485). An IMF structural adjustment program is a requirement for structural-adjustment lending by the Bank. These programs are pervasive in Africa. Since the early 1980s, forty African countries have been required to pursue structural adjustment programs as conditions for World Bank or IMF lending (Loxley 1990: 8). The general package of adjustment measures includes reductions in public spending, tax reform that includes reduced taxes on private business and increased consumption taxes, reduction of state ownership, making state-owned enterprises more efficient, deregulation of the economy, export promotion, and welcoming foreign investment (Sawyerr 1990: 221–222).

There is a vast literature on the effects of structural adjustment programs. There is also a growing body of literature on the effects of structural adjustment on women in Africa (Gladwin 1991; Elson 1992; Gallin and Ferguson 1991). This chapter is more concerned with demonstrating that the theoretical framing of the crisis facing African economies undertaken by the World Bank and the Southern Africa regional organization—the Southern African Development Coordination Conference (SADCC)—dovetails with theories of modernization and the African soft state to produce a thoroughly gendered version of the nature of the crisis confronting Africa and the solutions to the crisis.

▲ The World Bank's Modernization Theory

A number of writers have alluded to the World Bank's reliance on the modernization paradigm discussed in Chapter 2. Seidman (1989: 2) castigates the Bank for searching for national leaders in Africa who have the "'n-achievement' or entrepreneurial skills" for development. Bernstein (1990: 6) argues that the Bank's modernization framework, applied to agriculture, produces a two-pronged definition of development: technical progress and commoditization, or a combination of the "ideas about the development of technical conditions of production with ideas about the development of certain social conditions of production (that is markets, or simply *the* market)." In his trenchant analysis, Bernstein (1990: 9) maintains that the Bank seeks to concentrate resources in order to accelerate commoditization, a version of modernization theory's "trickle down theory" of development. According to Onimode (1989: 31) and many others (e.g., Harris 1989; Mbilinyi 1990), the World Bank programs increase dependence and integrate Third World countries more firmly into the world capitalist system. According to Harris (1989: 21), "the main role of the IMF and World Bank is the construction, regulation, and support of a world system where multinational corporations trade and move capital without restriction from national states."

Mackintosh (1990: 46) discusses how the Bank valorizes the market in a purely abstract, universal, and ahistorical manner. This is similar to Hyden's (1983b: 100) tendency to separate politics and the market and portray the market as a producer of rationality and efficiency. Hyden argues that the market is the most "powerful tool" to change institutions and behavior, encourages cost-benefit analysis considerations at the level of the household, and "is simpler and more flexible" (Hyden 1983b: 105).

Like modernization theorists, the World Bank stresses that state capacity and penetration are most effective when private enterprise and initiative are supported. The Bank is less concerned with the achievement of equality and more with the conditions that will allow free-market forces to "provide the appropriate engine for a resumption of economic growth and development" (Sawyerr 1990: 221).

Two key World Bank publications, issued in 1981 and 1989, have "strategic ideological significance" (Bernstein 1990: 16). They provide a comprehensive articulation of the overall philosophy guiding structural adjustment programs. Unlike other criticisms, the analysis that follows attempts to uncover the embedded ideas that link the Bank's definition of development with pervasively dichotomous gender oppositions. Thus, for example, while numerous writers have criticized the Bank's emphasis on the wonders of the market, no one has explored the implicit and gendered linkage between acquisitive individualism and constructions of modernity. While many critics have noted the invisibility of women in the formulation of World Bank policies, few have tried to argue that women do in fact, occupy a particular location in the Bank's schema for development in sub-Saharan Africa. Finally, while a number of important studies have examined the likely consequences of structural adjustment on food costs, poverty, education, and health, few have examined the likely consequences of structural adjustment and increased dependence on the operation of the contemporary African state.

▲ Themes of Accelerated Development

The World Bank's 1981 report, *Accelerated Development in Sub-Saharan Africa: An Agenda for Action*, attempts to rebut dependency theory's emphasis on external factors by devoting six pages in Chapter 3 to "External Factors," while devoting twenty-one pages to the "Policy Administrative Framework" in Chapter 4. The report criticizes four specific policies undertaken by postindependence African governments: trade and exchange rate policies, which are biased against agriculture; the context of economic decisionmaking, which is marked by a lack of efficiency; the lack of organization, along with weak management practices, especially in transport, construction, farming, and parastatals; and the burgeoning size of postindependence governments.

The recurrent theme of the report is that governments have inhibited the proper functioning of the market. In fact, in the report's liberal framework human society is depicted as a series of market relations. For example, in the context of a discussion about policy changes recommended for transport and communications, the task of government is specified as "maintaining a clear and stable legal and financial framework in which local initiative can flourish" (World Bank 1981: 106). The report praises small-scale informal irrigation schemes that have "been developed by the farming population with little, if any, help from governments" (World Bank 1981: 80). In criticizing government policies that hamper private traders, the report insists that governments should only make "markets more competitive through better information, roads, and marketing facilities [rather] than by acting as substitutes for traders" (World Bank 1981: 64). In other words, the sole task of government should be to provide a framework to promote and protect competition and the price mechanism, a classic liberal formulation (Lukes 1978: 93).

This is also similar to Hyden's (1983b: 129) call for the emergence of a more disciplined state rather than one that has stifled initiative and does not take costs, benefits, efficiency, and productivity into account. Juxtaposed with the dynamic and competitive market is the "personalized and particularistic" state that suffocates market and the rationality and instrumentality that accompany its operation. Markets are the most effective instruments of policy change (Hyden 1983b: 76).

What emerges from the 1981 report's analysis is a picture of rational economic man impeded by an overextended and "soft state." The "dynamic and highly competitive" private sector is constrained by a soft state (World Bank 1981: 37). At the center of the Bank's prescription for ailing African economies is the private farmer who owns a "few hectares more than the average" and who can "spearhead the introduction of new methods" in export agriculture (World Bank 1981: 52). And, while it has been established that in sub-Saharan Africa women engage in extensive farming activities, the farmer who is supposed to initiate new agricultural developments there is a male. In the 1981 report, women are mentioned approximately three times. The report notes that there are few women extension agents (1981: 74); that education for women is important (87); and that "equipment aimed at reducing the labor input of women's tasks" should be developed in order to "increase labor productivity in agriculture" (75). The stifled entrepreneur is the rational African farmer who will respond rationally to increases in producer prices, an actor

> whose very humanity is based on their independence from the will of others, and who may dispose of their own persons and capacities freely, since they owe nothing to the community as a whole, either for who they are or for the resources they possess (Hartsock 1983: 38–39).

The African farmer is presented as seeking independence from both the state and the household, as a subject who rationally obeys the market and who is capable of innovation only under conditions of intense competition with other farmers.

With this framework, a historical analysis of institutions becomes irrelevant. In fact, the 1981 report (1981: 86) argues that "there are some basic value-neutral skills and techniques that must be widely disseminated if government is to function effectively," as if donors need only pass along certain management and bureaucratic practices to African civil servants. To imply that internships with international institutions, which "will serve as instruments for managerial and technical training on the job," is what is needed to accelerate development is to underestimate the importance of political institutions, communities, and other sites of cooperation and conflict besides the market—such as the household.

In an interesting passage on education the report (World Bank 1981: 81) states that

> The impact of education extends beyond the traditional production sector into the household. Educated women, even if they do not participate in the labor force, can have a significant impact on the country's economy through lower fertility rates, health information, and more "household production."

The separation of the traditional sector from the household maintains rather than challenges the distinction between the public and private spheres. The public sphere is the world of markets and men, farmers who spearhead new production techniques beyond the watchful eye of an overbearing government. The household itself remains invisible. Women populate the "traditional" economy and the report winds up providing a few recommendations about the need to hire more female extension agents and devise labor-saving devices to women who work in the "traditional" sector.

On the other hand, as in Hyden, the attributes of the state resemble characteristics theoretically associated with females and tradition. Juxtaposed with the dynamic, innovative, competitive world of rational economic man is the overbearing, inefficient, particularistic, and personalistic soft state. The policies recommended by the Bank are intended to provide a defense against this state (and female) power.

▲ The 1989 Report: From Crisis to Sustainable Growth

A decade of political lobbying by environmental and women's groups is evident in the Bank's 1989 study, *Sub-Saharan Africa: From Crisis to Sustainable Growth*. Compared with the passing references to women in the 1981 report, women are discussed no less than twenty-five times a decade later, often in fairly lengthy passages that demonstrate some familiarity with the literature on women in development. In a further attempt to address its critics, the report also discusses the need to protect the most vulnerable members of society from the effects of structural adjustment programs and the need to tailor structural adjustment to a particular country's circumstances rather than relying on wholesale adoption of a standardized package (World Bank 1989: 36, 73). The Economic Commission for Africa (UNECA 1989: 19), for example, chastised the Bank for "indiscriminate and doctrinaire" privatization policies. The Bank's 1989 report (1989: 194) thus calls for a "new international compact for Africa" and an effort "to seek the highest ground for joint action" (World Bank 1989: 14) in an attempt to absorb criticism and present its recommendations in a positive light.

Despite an attempt to respond to critics, the 1989 report continues the major theme of the 1981 report in the "unrelenting anti-statism of its core discourse" (Bernstein 1990: 19). Like the 1981 Berg report, *Sustainable Growth* prescribes a minimal role for the state: it is both "an uninspired entrepreneur and a bad manager" (World Bank 1989: 38). The state's role should be to establish

> a predictable and honest administration of the regulatory framework, to assure law and order, and to foster a stable, objective, and transparent judicial system. In addition it should provide reliable and efficient infrastructure and social and information services—all preconditions for the efficiency of productive enterprises, whether private or state owned (World Bank 1989: 55).

This liberal and minimalist state is what will create an "enabling environment" to "reward efficiency and innovation" and "release private energies and encourage initiative at every level" (World Bank 1989: 4–5, 8, 59). Government should remove distortions against agriculture and then assume its rightful "neutral" role and allow farmers to be guided by their "comparative advantage" (World Bank 1989: 92).

The chief engine of development is again the African entrepreneur: an entire chapter of the 1989 report is devoted to entrepreneurship. In 1960, Rostow (1960: 50) argued that "take-off" required the existence of some group that is prepared to accept innovation: "adequate entrepreneurship" is the key factor, along with "a whole catalogue of necessary social change" that Rostow poses as a series of challenges:

> How to persuade the peasant to change his methods and shift to producing for wider markets; how to build up a corps of technicians, capable of manipulating new techniques; how to create a corps of entrepreneurs . . . under a regime of regular technological change and obsolescence; how to create a modern professional civil and military service . . . oriented to the welfare of the nation and to standards of efficient performance, rather than to graft and to ties of family, clan, or region (Rostow 1960: 140).

The 1989 report restates Rostow's assessment of the challenge of take-off: "To make progress every country needs a technocratic elite of entrepreneurs, civil servants, administrators, academics, and other professionals. Although few in number, they will be important catalysts for development" (World Bank 1989: 54). While it is clear that Rostow had a group of forward-looking men in mind (see Chapter 2), the Bank's language is usually more inclusive and envisions women's integration into this corps of catalysts for development. The activity described as a requisite for development, however, continues to define it as a distinctively masculinist activity. Progress, freedom, and development are defined in terms of skilled personnel who are conversant in the application of modern technology and science to nature and who are free to direct their energies to that end. What is valued in development is what historically has defined the world of public man. While Rostow explicitly juxtaposes efficient performance against family and clan, the gendered dichotomies of the World Bank report are more subtle but just as important: the catalysts for change and development are those who are free from private power and the pull of the household.

Like Hyden (1985: 201), the Bank also extols the virtues of city life and links it with the development of the requisite modern attitudes so carefully outlined by Inkeles and Smith in their study of the emergence of modern men:

> Cities foster modernization and change and consequently are the nerve centers of the development process. . . . Rapidly expanding urban centers are crucibles of acculturation to modernity and to the market economy (World Bank 1989: 43, 49).

In an interesting revision of modernization theory's (and Hyden's) assumptions about the superiority of city life, the Bank argues that in Africa cities have not developed in the "appropriate" manner. Urban areas in Africa are characterized as overcrowded, inefficiently run, and are populated by people who benefit from low food prices and government subsidies (World Bank 1989: 43). The balance should be restored by favoring farmers in the rural areas who, through production of export crops, can earn the requisite foreign exchange to begin an orderly process of industrialization and urbanization.

The report (World Bank 1989: 90) argues that the two priorities for agriculture should be incentives for the private sector and harnessing technology in order to improve agricultural growth to 4 percent a year. The marriage of private initiative and technology is portrayed as the most effective development strategy for Africa. As Rostow (1960: 26) noted over thirty years ago, modernization requires that "men must become prepared for a life of change and specialized function." And, as Hyden (1983a: 80) argues, "the bourgeoisie is an indispensable agent of progress."

The World Bank's approach to understanding the economic crisis in Africa is thus firmly anchored in the dichotomies of city/countryside, modern/traditional, bourgeois/feudal, and individual/collective, which have played such a pervasive role in theorizing about political development by modernization and soft-state theorists. The categories are fundamentally gendered, with the latter concepts linked to women's nature-bound activities and in opposition to the dynamic and everchanging public realm. Political development, according to these theorists, takes place beyond the realm of stagnant tradition. As the 1989 report (World Bank 1989: 38) states, "In the most fundamental sense development depends on the capacity to initiate, sustain, and accommodate change."

The fact that some attention is given to African women farmers in the 1989 report does not alter this basic framing of development issues. In one of the lengthier passages that discusses women, the report (1989: 86) recognizes that "'modernization' has shifted the balance of advantage against women," and it chronicles the ways in which women are disadvantaged in terms of land rights, access to credit, technology, extension services, and education: "as a result, women are less well equipped to take advantage of the better income-earning opportunities in Africa." The Bank's prescription is to exhort the state to "enable women to play their full role in economic and social development," to "remove the innumerable obstacles to the true fulfillment of [women's] potential," and to "reach both genders effectively" (World Bank 1989: 15, 34, 65).

At the same time, the state is instructed to play a "neutral" role and to provide a minimal regulatory framework that protects property and enforces commercial contracts (World Bank 1989: 9). What is the explanation for the Bank's call for a greater role for women in development while at the same time insisting that the state is "bad at picking winners" (World Bank 1989: 173) and should take a neutral stance toward various competing interests? Feminist theories of the liberal state are useful in illuminating the contradictions in the Bank's formulation of "the woman question" in capitalist development.

Brown (1992: 13–14) has suggested a number of masculine dimensions of state power in her analysis of the contemporary United States that, somewhat modified, are useful in understanding the functioning of the state in contemporary Africa. First, although the ruling classes in the contemporary African state lack the hegemony of the ruling classes in industrialized capitalist states, the state nevertheless possesses a capitalist dimension that privileges private property rights (Brown 1992: 13). Second, the contemporary African state has a liberal dimension as well in that "ideology, legislation, and adjudication are predicated upon a division of the polity into the ostensibly autonomous spheres of family, civil society (economy), and state" (Brown 1992: 17). Finally, the contemporary African state has a bureaucratic dimension: "bureaucratic hierarchalism, proceduralism, and the cult of expertise" constitute an important aspect of contemporary state activity. As Fatton (1989a: 176) has argued, contra the soft-state approach, the African state is the "unsteady state of a dominant class that has yet to become hegemonic." The recommendations of the World Bank can be viewed as policies that simultaneously reinforce the capitalist, liberal, and bureaucratic aspects of the African state while at the same time reinforcing, in general, masculine privilege.

▲ The Capitalist Dimension

The World Bank's recommendations do not challenge the division of labor in which men do "productive" work while women do unpaid reproductive work, a key aspect of the masculinism of the capitalist state (Brown 1992: 20). The report never challenges the continued performance of unpaid labor by women; it recommends that women be provided "tools, food processing equipment or services (such as corn-milling), and devices to lighten household work, which would release more time for agricultural production and other income-generating activity" (World Bank 1989: 113). While recommending that women engage in income-generating activity, the report also continues to emphasize women's "traditional" role within the household and recommends the utilization of time-saving devices such as more abundant water supplies, to relax "some of the constraints on women in their household nurturing capacity" (World Bank 1989: 87). As Elson (1992: 34) notes, the costs of structural adjustment are shifted to the unpaid economy. Women are called upon to bear the costs of capitalist state policies by generating more income. Meanwhile, they are expected to continue their sex-specific nurturing activities within the household. In this sense, the Bank's recipe for higher rates of capital accumulation, its "unitary and inclusive vision of market opportunity" (Bernstein 1990: 19), rests on masculinist foundations that rely on continued unpaid labor in the home and increased wage-work for women in the transition to "development."[1]

▲ The Liberal Dimension

As Okin (1979) and Jagger (1983) have shown, liberal theory casts the family as natural with the male as head of family, rather than the adult human individual as the fundamental subject (Okin 1979: 201). The Bank proposes that private land rights be more firmly established and that medium- and large-scale farms be given more incentives (World Bank 1989: 93). At the same time, the report treats women's role in economic development as a problem of access and opportunity. The implicit liberal assumption is that women are the same as men but are barred from equal opportunity by old-fashioned customs and laws that can easily be swept away. Furthermore, questions about the state's role in reproduction, child-care, and housework are not asked because the liberal imperative is to move women beyond the household: women should be more like men. The family is thus depoliticized and "so is women's situation and women's work within it" (Brown 1992: 17). Therefore, the rights conferred upon women in the public sphere by liberal modernization theory's strategy can only be partially realized, because the "natural" realm of the family is excluded from political analysis. As Elson (1989: 63) argues,

Access to markets has benefits for women, but those benefits are always limited, even if markets are entirely free of gender discrimination. They are limited because the reproduction and maintenance of human resources is structured by unequal gender relations, and because the reproduction and maintenance of human resources cannot be directly and immediately responsive to market signals.

Furthermore, even if women were supplied with laborsaving devices in order to realize more income beyond the traditional sector, user fees for water, sanitation, education, and health disproportionately affect women as "lead managers" (World Bank 1989: 86) of the household who are often the ones who must obtain these basic resources.

▲ The Bureaucratic Dimension

In its efforts to seek autonomy, penetration, extraction of resources, and legitimation (Forrest 1988: 423), the African state attempts to implement policies that increase bureaucratic control. There are numerous examples of state efforts to augment bureaucratic power, ranging from the establishment of agricultural marketing boards in order to control export crops to nationalization and numerous reforms of central-local government relations in order to strengthen the state's bureaucratic apparatus.

The programs promulgated by the World Bank appear to be aimed at swollen bureaucracies. The Bank recommends freeing the market and devolving power from the state to grassroots and nongovernmental organizations, including women's groups (World Bank 1989: 6). On the other hand, implementation of many of the recommendations in fact ensure the further bureaucratization of economic and social life. For example, the Bank favors secure private land rights in order to deliver the requisite technology to farmers who can spearhead the new production techniques; but delivery of this technology would certainly require a new layer of bureaucratic expertise. The Bank also argues that governments can enhance their efficiency if taxes on trade are replaced with taxes on consumers and user fees applied to a range of services, from water-use and sanitation to education (World Bank 1989: 6, 86).

In the Bank's scenario, women would become the "targets" of these new policies delivered by a more disciplined bureaucracy for structural adjustment:

> Women farmers should be involved in on-farm research to make sure that the new varieties and technologies recommended largely

> correspond to their needs and constraints. . . . Women's groups
> need to be fostered. They could then be used, for instance, not only
> as contacts for extension services but also for channeling credit for
> the purchase of inputs. Finally, female education needs to be ex-
> panded, since farmers with higher levels of education have been
> shown to achieve higher increases in output from new technology
> (1989: 104).

Given that women's "household nurturing" capacities have often remained intact, and that spending on health-care and education have
decreased, this bureaucratic dimension of structural adjustment
would allow the state to develop new means of control over women's
lives while ensuring that they bear a large share of the costs of structural adjustment.

It is in this light that the 1989 report's interesting references to
"indigenous African values and institutions" and how they can support development strategies should be examined: "communal culture, the participation of women in the economy, respect for nature—all these can be used in constructive ways" (World Bank 1989:
60). In this formulation, women, the informal sector, and the "community" occupy one side of a dichotomous framework; on the other
side are the modern sector, entrepreneurial farmers, and the "private sector." The Bank thus calls upon the informal ("traditional")
sector to absorb the painful costs of adjustment. In a sense, this portrayal differs from that of early modernization theorists, whose dualistic framework insisted on the necessity of overcoming and moving
beyond traditional society. The 1989 report casts women and the informal sector as the "safety net" in the transition to a modern, productive, capitalist economy. Hyden, too, takes this approach in some
of his later writing. For example, Hyden (1990: 262) has recognized
the persistence of the economy of affection and suggests that a compromise of sorts be struck between the state and this economy. The
state should "provide space" to the economy of affection in order to
"broaden its linkages and productive capacity as new opportunities
arise." The "primordial" or "god-given" realm, which is the "natural
world over which human beings have little control," can be an important site for the generation of compliance and trust, which in
turn can promote political development. Hyden and Peters (1991:
322) also take the Bank's position that "market penetration may *open
up* new opportunities for women that were not there before," and the
market "does provide an opportunity for women to get an alternative
source of income."

These reformulations of the role that tradition can play in the
transition to modernity are significant: they offer a more comprehensive view of women's role in the "traditional" economy and

informal sector and at the same time maintain a distinction between the "natural" private realm of family and household and a public realm that transcends the "rudimentary and narrow" relations of the primordial realm. A recognition of women's economic role while simultaneously maintaining hierarchical distinctions between private/public, traditional/modern, and female/male is likely to enhance the masculine moorings of the liberal, capitalist, and bureaucratic dimensions of the African state. Structural adjustment thus represents a more sophisticated and reformulated version of modernization theory. Edwards (1989: 129) argues that, for the World Bank, "participation" is actually seen as a mechanism of cost-recovery in projects, reducing costs incurred by governments, and improving the accuracy of research by outside agencies, none of which is truly participatory. While adopting the language of participation and local control, it is an approach that promises enhanced control, bureaucracy, and discipline over women's lives.

▲ The Woman Question in SADCC

Regional integration has been promoted by the World Bank, the Economic Commission for Africa (ECA), and a number of academics. The 1989 World Bank report cites the benefits of integration as leading to the development of "regional centers of excellence" to pool resources, the enhancement of food security, new markets for underutilized industry, and the more efficient exploration of energy sources (World Bank 1989: 148). The U.N. Economic Commission for Africa (UNECA 1989: 13) criticizes the balkanization of the continent by colonialists as a deplorable legacy and foresees regional integration as a means of realizing economies of scale, enabling countries to pool resources, and generate backward and forward linkages in industrial development. Seidman (1989: 19) states that the development of pole-of-growth industries could "initiate integrated self-reliant regional development" in Southern Africa and reduce dependence on Western capital and the conditions laid down by the IMF and the World Bank.

SADCC was formed by nine independent states in southern Africa (in 1980, by Angola, Botswana, Malawi, Mozambique, Swaziland, Tanzania, Zambia, Zimbabwe; joined in 1989 by Namibia) to lessen dependence on South Africa and to combine resources and expertise in applying for foreign aid and investment. Each member-country is responsible for a particular sector and develops projects, requests external aid, and disseminates information to member-states. Angola, for example, is responsible for the energy sector,

Botswana for agricultural research, and so forth. Gender and women's issues is not designated as one of the covered sectors. In 1987 the council reported that it saw no need to have an independent sector for women-in-development issues (SADCC 1987: 6).

It is estimated that between 25 and 40 percent of households in the region (which has a population of 70 million) are headed by women (SADCC 1986: 6). SADCC, whose initial major projects focused on the rehabilitation of transport and communications, has, however, addressed the question of the part of women in development. Given the increasing recognition of the importance of regional cooperation and integration, especially in Southern Africa, it is important to examine the way in which gender and women have been theorized by SADCC. In general, it has tended to frame "women and development" issues in ways similar to the World Bank.

In an outline of the challenges faced by women in agriculture, the 1986 proceedings of a meeting of some SADCC members acknowledged that women have less access to money, education, credit, and extension services (SADCC 1986: 4). At the SADCC annual conference in 1991 (1991: 7), the proceedings restate the central challenge of including women in development projects, which is a major World Bank theme as well:

> Women have to be brought more fully into the development process and the legal, social, and economic barriers to their full participation in development removed. They must have equal access to land, credit, extension services, education, and training. Their special needs must be catered for, if further productivity gains are to result from their efforts.

This passage is a concise restatement of the liberal underpinnings of modernization theory. The differences in the process of male and female modernization is seen as a problem of diffusion (Jaquette 1982: 269) and the household, as the "natural" location of women, is not discussed. SADCC also takes an interest-group approach as a strategy for integrating women's issues into development projects. The account of the 1986 proceedings recommends that national women's organizations and ministries should develop liaisons with SADCC and that the various sectors of SADCC should appoint specialists to "integrate various women's issues into development" (SADCC 1986: 18).

Although the SADCC reports do not emphasize the need to increase women's productivity as much as the World Bank, there is some recognition that discrimination against women has hampered efficiency and productivity in agriculture. The 1986 report recommended that women's role in the economy be addressed through the provision of female extension workers, more credit, clearer explanations of policy choices for women, and training in the installation of water systems (SADCC 1986: 26–30). •

This framing of "the woman question" in agricultural development in Southern Africa is a familiar counterpart to World Bank and modernization theory. It rests upon a hierarchical structuring of the public and private worlds. In SADCC documents, the household is at one level rendered invisible because the task of development is framed as one of bringing women into the public sphere, where development takes place. On the other hand, the labor of women in the "traditional" economy is regarded as important, and recommendations have been made to introduce laborsaving devices for women in their roles as "lead managers" in the household. A 1989 report (SADCC 1989: 12) stated that planning for technology and SADCC projects should take these "peculiar needs" of women into account. For example, the development of water sources close to human settlements, improvements in animal-driven transport, and the development of feeder roads to promote local trade do not challenge the household division of labor: if implemented, they would often increase the work of women.

SADCC's formulation of women and development issues undoubtedly reflects the influence that Western donors have had on the content of regional development programs. Western countries in fact encouraged the formation of SADCC as a means of diverting confrontation with South Africa (Amin 1987: 8). Dependence on donors—in part deepened because of continued destabilization from South Africa—has produced a similar definition of modernization and development by national governments and international donors. Pan-Africanist delegates to a 1988 SADCC conference on women and food technologies in the region recommended programs to sensitize men to gender issues and to recognize the cultural constraints to women's full participation in political and social life (SADCC 1988: 10). This suggestion could constitute the beginning of a recognition of the sexual division of labor in the household and the importance of understanding its dynamics. Until SADCC moves beyond its narrow definition of production, modernization, and development, it will continue to perpetuate, along with very powerful international donors, underdevelopment for a large proportion of Southern Africa's population.

▲ Conclusion

Nearly thirty-five years ago, McClelland (1976: 210–233) extolled the virtues of entrepreneurial activity: risk-taking, energy and innovation, individual responsibility, and knowledge about the results of action were defined as the essence of entrepreneurship. The history of Western capitalism was defined as the "history of the owner-entrepreneur who did everything for himself" (McClelland 1976: 229). Today, theorists of the African soft state bemoan the absence of entrepreneurs: "Because peasant producers employ rudimentary technologies and accumulate meager economic surpluses, African societies do not automatically give birth to capitalist classes or elaborate state structures of their own" (Bratton 1989: 410). Only capitalist development can prompt the emergence of entrepreneurs, risk-takers who are eager to innovate and adapt to the everchanging facets of urban life (and the increasingly technologically sophisticated requisites of farming). Such developments require a minimalist state, one that does not "pick winners" but rather establishes an "enabling environment" and the incentives to innovate to farmers and firms (World Bank 1989: 6). This portrayal of development as something that is achieved by individual men who are unencumbered by the demands of traditional society is a distinctive view of what it means to be modern. Separation from the household, detachment from "traditional" relationships, autonomy from the old order, and subordination of these former attachments to a new order that values acquisitive behavior, rationality, and independence, is a view of modernity that powerfully joins liberalism and constructions of masculinity. It is a vision that insists that modernity be realized beyond the realm of the household, necessity, and tradition.

Like the SSRC framework, the World Bank's prescription for Africa would produce more specialization and hierarchy, despite the emphasis on allowing market forces to operate without bureaucratic interference. Africa's escape from economic crisis to sustainable growth, as described by the Bank, will require pervasive regulation and more bureaucracy to monitor the privatization of land rights, the provision of agricultural inputs, and the delivery of new technologies. The effects of enhanced regulation on the lives of women is hinted at in the Bank's vision of how women's groups could be used as targets of enhanced regulatory power and as important new beneficiaries of the enabling environment created by state policies. In language that hints at the important function of "control through participation" as described by Edwards (1989: 129), the Bank (1989: 45) describes the challenge faced by African governments as one of "first, how to make the poor more productive, and second, how to provide productive assets to the poor." The poor can be made more productive only if they become recipients and targets of government policy. As long as participation remains a form of control by international donors who set the agenda, such policies will not necessarily lead to "empowerment" (another term employed by the 1989 report).

As Wolin (1960: 364) has explained, enhanced organization "signifies a method of social control, a means of imparting order, structure, and regularity to society." Alongside bourgeois man (Prometheus, in Hyden's language) stands a new organizational structure that promises to deliver the African state from the social chaos of tradition, the economy of affection, and the household. It is unlikely that bourgeois man in concert with a hardened state will create a "woman-friendly" polity (Jones 1990).

The Bank's more recent formulations that highlight the informal sector and women's role within it and Hyden's praise for the reciprocity and trust that flourish within the economy of affection do not challenge the dualistic framework upon which the masculinism of liberal modernization rests. The "safety net" role of these structures still constitute a way station in the transition to capitalist modernity. New state policies designed to organize, discipline, and regulate the household will ensure that women will bear much of the cost of structural adjustment.

It is no surprise that the framing of the crisis of African development and prescriptions for achieving sustainable growth by powerful international donor organizations has influenced the way in which "the woman question" and development have been formulated within SADCC. A separation of the traditional/private sphere from the modern/public sphere has led to calls for bringing women into development, which implicitly is defined as the world of markets, rationality, and productivity. "Women's work" in the economy is treated as an unproductive sector that needs to be made more efficient. Thus, echoing the World Bank, SADCC's goal with regard to women is an effort to foster modernization in the "traditional" economy and improve women's conditions there.

Some of the literature on Women in Development (WID) can also can be located in a tradition of theorizing about development that does not question the framework of the market. Kardam (1990; 1991), for example, explores how the World Bank's organizational mission, bureaucratic structure, and reliance on the criteria of productivity and efficiency ensure resistance to WID issues. She emphasizes the need for internal pressures for change within the World Bank, the emergence of committed leadership, and efforts to develop more effective compliance mechanisms as the chief means by which development for women can be achieved. Kardam's analysis does not really question the likelihood of that women will be integrated into a development blueprint anchored in efforts to achieve technical mastery over the environment and geared toward greater productivity and efficiency (Kardam 1991: 117). As Ferguson (1990: 229) puts it, such an approach would "view development itself as a problem, questioning the foundation of the development enterprise."

The most significant challenge to theories of liberal capitalist de-velopment has been dependency theory. Like soft-state theory and its World Bank counterpart, dependency theory has found expression in revolutions in a number of Third World settings, including South-ern Africa. The next two chapters explore theoretical and practical expressions of dependency and revolution.

▲ Notes

1. The work on the effects of structural adjustment in specific national contexts confirms that this capitalist dimension of the state plays a powerful role in defining "women's work." In Tanzania, Tripp (1992: 165) reports that urban women dramatically increased their pursuit of income generating pro-jects in addition to childrearing and housework in response to the declines in real wages that accompanied structural adjustment. Marshall (1990: 33) reports that the same kinds of demands have been placed on women farm-ers in Mozambique, who also must negotiate a livelihood in the midst of war.

▲ 5
Marxism, Masculinity, and Dependency Theory

We saw in Chapter 2 that early theorists of modernization conceived of it essentially in masculinist terms. Prescriptions by modernization theorists were designed to overcome what was perceived implicitly as female-headed "backward" households that embodied social relations and structures that challenged male prerogatives and provided a powerful antidote to modernity (and capitalism).

Dependency theory, which emerged first in Latin America and then was "consumed" in the United States (Cardoso 1977), appeared to challenge the entire dualistic structure upon which modernization theory rested. Modernization, for dependency theorists, was in fact the spread of capitalism around the globe, a "'rapacious' stage in the history of capitalism which intensifies the exploitation of the imperialized formation while augmenting the process of accumulation by the more advanced bourgeoisies of the imperialist countries" (Ahmad 1983: 33).

Nevertheless dependency theory, particularly its U.S. variant, never challenged the dynamism and inherently progressive characteristics of capitalism. While there have been vehement debates about the origins of capitalism, the forms of resistance it is most likely to generate, and its likely effects on Third World societies, virtually all schools of thought within dependency theory have represented capitalism as a dynamic, rational, and technologically superior phenomenon, an emblem of the gradual realization of an end to material necessity. This image is presented mainly through juxtaposing capitalist modernity with "unproductive" sectors of society. In this sense, dependency theorists retained a conception of the traditional private and modern public spheres, but recast the terms of the debate by portraying indigenous peoples as victims of capitalism. Although women are invisible in most of the classic dependency theory texts, in the practice of revolutionary governments concerned with "the woman question" women are presented as victims who are doubly

oppressed by colonial capitalism and the "backward" and "unproductive" practices that inhibit their full participation in public life.
Thus, dependency theory shares with Marxism a blind spot about
gender and, as with modernization theory, its concerns about development derive from a masculinist preoccupation with constructions
of a rationalized public sphere. More concretely, the contradictions
of this masculinist framework are evident in the policies undertaken
by revolutionary governments in Southern Africa. After the exploration in this chapter of the philosophical underpinnings of dependency theory, delineating its commonalities with Marxist theory,
Chapter 6 will explore how the "woman question" has been treated
in Angola and Mozambique.

▲ "Masculine Marx" and Dependency Theory

Dependency theory's debt to Marxism[1] has been traced elsewhere
(Cardoso 1977; Randall and Theobald 1985: ch. 4). One of the many
insights of dependency theory was that benign depictions of the
forces of modernization by modernization theorists (i.e., aid and
trade) masked imperial interests and disguised the continuation of
neocolonial exploitative relations between center and periphery. Like
Marx, dependency theorists effectively demonstrated that the inter-
state system created an illusion of equality between nations when in
fact those relations were governed by domination and exploitation.

However, while dependency theorists argue that the causes of
stagnation lie with external rather than domestic forces, they nevertheless treat dependent societies much as Marx treated Asiatic and
primitive societies. Marx attributed the stagnation of the Asiatic
mode of production to a number of factors, including the absence of
private property, the low level of productive forces, and the disper-
sion of villages, all of which blocked the growth of "opposing tensions" (Melotti 1977: 57). For dependency theorists, precapitalist social formations, along with international capitalism, are often also
portrayed as "obstructions" to the realization of truly autonomous
development in the periphery. Although Marx recognized that "dy-
nastic upheavals, revolts, invasions, divisions, and reunification" occurred in Asiatic societies, they took place within the "airy region of
politics" and did not mark significant changes in material life
(Melotti 1977: 107). Likewise, Charney (1987: 48) emphasizes the
continuity of postindependence politics in Africa: "The position of
the dominated classes, the power of foreign capital and the international division of labor have changed little since independence," because of the nature of the postcolonial state.

Both traditions also rely on implicit comparisons between capitalist/modern and precapitalist/Asiatic or primitive societies. While the former possess an inherent capacity for independent development, the latter societies are exploited, incomplete, and disarticulated. As Medley (1989: 86–87) notes, Samir Amin, a leading dependency theorist, builds an explanation of dependent development that posits that the center created the periphery as its *complementary* opposite (emphasis in the original). In this sense, the model of development held by dependency theorists shares with modernization theorists a conception of Third World societies that rests on dichotomous oppositions between the rational sphere of social production and the private precapitalist realm. This "structuring of paired opposites" effectively displaces the "subordinate term beyond the boundary of what is significant and desirable" (Gregory 1989: xvi). Just as dichotomies such as nature/culture, reason/emotion, subject/object, and order/anarchy have shaped the construction of modernization theory, the binary logic of center/periphery, with the latter term complementary and subordinate, has served as an anchor to conceptualizations of dependency, underdevelopment, and liberation.

A second and related theme of dependency theory is its portrayal of industry and industrialization as the paradigm of economic development and the solution to the problem of dependency. Industrialization and the autonomy that purportedly accompanies it constitutes the realm of freedom for dependency theorists. Precapitalist structures, on the other hand, are usually treated in one of two ways. At times its inhabitants are depicted as victims of the spread of capitalist relations of production: the "reserve army of labor" or the "unproductive masses" are characterized as survivors of the operation of transnational corporations, foreign aid projects, and exploitative trade relations. At other times precapitalist social structures are depicted as obstructions to the realization of effective challenges to dependency. For Charney (1987: 52) precapitalist ideologies of legitimation are based on hierarchy and the subordination of various groups, "youths and women must efface themselves before older men, serfs and vassals before their lords, talibes before marabouts [religious leader and follower]." This implicitly juxtaposes a dynamic sphere of public, social, and industrial production with the precapitalist "realm of necessity" and renders the latter sphere a "mere" site of victimization and subordination of "women and youths"; and as such, not the focus of sustained political analysis. This dichotomous presentation of the rationalized, efficient sphere of capitalism with the stagnant precapitalist social formation produces in dependency theory a gender-biased account of the causes and consequences of dependency. Dependency theory, following Marx, sets out from

men's labor, ignores the specificity of women's labor, and fails to recognize the importance of social conflicts other than class conflicts
(Hartsock 1983: 146).

The third tenet shared by Marxism and dependency theory is the
link made between freedom and the transcendence of necessity with
control over nature and the "exclusion of 'woman' from privileged
rationality, transcendence, and autonomy" (Peterson 1992: 202). Dependency theory shares with Marxism a tendency to define development as the successful struggle to master and transform nature
which, according to Balbus (1982: 17–18) has two consequences.
First, it leads to a conceptualization of all struggles as centered
around productive activity—thus excluding struggles between men
and women rather than man and nature. Second, the basis of human
freedom is the "ability to overcome the otherness of nature by making it into an extension of ourselves" (Balbus 1982: 18). Although dependency theorists are never explicit in linking women with nature,
their approach rests upon structured binary oppositions between
modern-capitalist/culture and traditional-precapitalist/nature that
are in turn anchored in essentialized gender differences.

▲ The Traditional, the Modern, and Dependency Theory

Andre Gundar Frank, in a scathing critique of modernization theory,
challenges the use of pattern variables for understanding development and underdevelopment (Frank 1969a). He argues that many
modernization theorists "associate particularism, ascription, and dif-
fuseness in underdevelopment with the family, the primitive tribe,
the folk community, the traditional sector of a dual society, and with
the underdeveloped countries and participation of the world in general" (Frank 1969a: 33). His quarrel, however, does not lie with the
characterization of "traditional" societies but rather with what causes
tradition to flourish. As he notes in another work:

> Economic development and underdevelopment are not just relative
> and quantitative, in that one represents more economic develop-
> ment than the other; economic development and underdevelop-
> ment are relational and qualitative, in that each is structurally
> different from, yet caused by its relation with, the other. Yet devel-
> opment and underdevelopment are the same in that they are the
> product of a single, but dialectically contradictory, economic struc-
> ture and process of capitalism (Frank 1969a: 9).

While this formulation is indeed dialectical and demonstrates the
compelling nature of Frank's approach, he retains a dichotomous

view of the difference between tradition and moderni
intent is to conceive of dependency as relational, devel
underdevelopment are in fact presented in theoretically
fied terms.

This reductionism is evident in the way Frank and ot
dency theorists differentiate development from underde\ ..opment.
According to Frank (1972: 13), the regions of the world that appear
the most underdeveloped are the ones that had the greatest ties with
capitalism in the past, until they were "abandoned by the metropolis
when for one reason or another business fell off." Amin (1982: 207)
also contends that stagnation and retrogression occurred in the peripheral economy at the time it became less important to the world
capitalist system. The capitalist sector of the satellite economy is its
"nerve and substance" (Frank 1969b: 22). The very dualism that
Frank and others reject is maintained in dependency theory because,
according to Frank, the inevitable polarization of classes that accompanies capitalism creates an increasing number of "essentially unproductive" masses in the satellite (Frank 1969b: 22). The productive
sector is the modern sector and the unproductive sector is the traditional. As Cardoso (1977: 7) points out, the essential binary oppositions (common in modernization theory) are retained: "dependency
and development, exploitation and wealth, backwardness and sophisticated technology, unemployment and extreme concentration
of income."

Samir Amin (1973: 66) utilizes the same dualistic framework in
his discussion of the exhaustion of the Ivory Coast "economic miracle." He effectively demonstrates that international specialization in
export crops and minerals, balkanization of the region by colonial
powers, and a postindependence growth strategy that relies upon extensive foreign investment has created crises in the budgets and balance of payments. However, his mechanistic account reproduces the
contrast paradigm of tradition and modernity: "The Ivory Coast is
certainly no longer the primitive country that it was in 1950. But it
has become a true underdeveloped country; well integrated, like its
elder neighbor Senegal, into the world capitalist economy" (1973:
66). Amin notes that the chiefly planter class continued to wield
power in the rural areas because of the "stubborn survival of various
elements of the traditional animist religion" (1973: 62). He describes
Mauritainia as a "country sunk in lethargy" until mining interests "set
off brutal social changes" (1973: 78). Guinean agriculture is described as "backward" (1973: 91).

Frank and other dependency theorists display the same sense of
awe and admiration, mixed with horror, at the capacity of capitalism
to transform social relations in Third World countries. Dependency

literature is replete with images of the increasing rationalization, concentration, and centralization of capital, and the growing impoverishment of marginalized workers. For example, Johnson (1972: 95), in discussing the power of transnational corporations, the IMF, and the World Bank, argues: "This is not a conspiracy. The policies of international lenders are rational and flow from the structure of the international system." Superior technology and abundant capital ensure that "national class and power systems mesh smoothly with the international system" (Johnson 1972: 105).

Brenner (1977) has argued that much of dependency theory is highly mechanistic and deterministic, especially with regard to the causes of class formation. The model of human behavior used by dependency theorists assumes the "extra-historical universe of *homo oeconomicas*, of individual profit maximizers competing on the market, outside of any system of social relations of exploitation" (Brenner 1977: 58). Thus, although dependency theory refutes the optimism of modernization theorists, it nevertheless is "neo-Smithian" because it retains many of the individualistic and mechanistic presuppositions held by Smith.

This variant of dependency theory abandons Marx's insistence on viewing history and the development of capitalism dialectically. Instead, while it conceives of capitalism as the inevitable and complete incorporation of all social formations into the world capitalist system, it also reproduces the dichotomies upon which modernization theory depends. International capitalism produces, in Johnson's (1972: 73) words, "national businessmen [who] grew up with and benefited from their nation's position as *de facto* colonies" and, in the words of Frank (1969b: 136), in Latin America an Indian class that is defined by its "status of inferiority, exploitation, poverty, and lack of culture." Amin (1982: 205) uses similar dichotomous imagery when he describes a developed economy as an "integrated whole" and the underdeveloped economy as "not integrated" and "disarticulated." Developed economies constitute a "true, structured, national economic space," while the "centers of gravity of the underdeveloped economy lie in the centers of the capitalist world."

Of course, Amin and other dependency theorists differ from modernization theorists in that they reject the "dualist" thesis of a modern and traditional sector in the dependent economy. Instead, dependency theorists conceive of the two sectors as integrally related, and "aggression by the capitalist mode of production from the outside . . . constitutes the essence of the problem of their transitions to formations of peripheral capitalism" (Amin 1974b: 142). While this formulation differs from that of modernization theory, the rationalized, modern, capitalist sphere remains privileged while the traditional sector is viewed as unproductive and an "obstruction" to the development of an economy with its own "independent dynamism" (Amin 1974b: 32, 35–36). As Mkandawire (1983: 53) aptly describes Amin's framework, "social formations of the peripheries consist of modern capitalist structures and deformed pre-capitalist structures." Thus, dependency theory's characterizations of capitalist and precapitalist formations, while appearing to challenge modernization on one level, actually conforms to its fundamental yet implicit gendered categories. The "deformed" precapitalist social structure is also the site of household production, wifehood, and motherhood.

▲ Gender and Dependency Theory

Neither gender nor women are explicitly discussed by the early dependency theorists. Frank (1969b: 17), for example, in his discussion of the variety of metropolitan-satellite domestic relationships that mirror international relations of dominance and subordination, never mentions the household:

> There are a variety of these metropolis-satellite relationships . . . between the latifundia and the minifundia surrounding it; between the owner or administrator-operated part of the latifundia enterprise and its dependent sharecropper or other tenant-run enterprises; even between a tenant farmer (or enterprise) and the permanent or occasional hired labor he may use; and of course, between each set of metropolises or each set of satellites up and down this chain.

Amin (1973: 63), in his analysis of the outward-directed growth strategy of the Ivory Coast, describes its class structure as consisting of rich planters and an agricultural proletariat in the rural areas; urban workers, artisans, small traders, and minor government and commercial workers in the urban areas; middle-rank officials; and, a "pseudo-bourgeoisie" of fewer than two thousand heads of families. Amin (1973: 160) mentions women once in *Neo-Colonialism in West Africa* (he estimates that 0.6 percent of the female population in Senegal speaks French).

What explains this invisibility of women in the dependency framework of analysis? At least part of the answer can be found in looking at dependency theory's roots in radical liberal and classical Marxist ideas concerning history and progress that prevailed in the nineteenth century (Molyneux 1991: 52). As Brenner (1977: 82) notes, dependency theorists conceive of the world's producers as individuals who are able, through their own egoistic motivations, to implement the most effective techniques of exploitation. Like Marx, Walter Rodney (1981: 3) emphasizes that human development implies "increased skill and capacity, greater freedom, creativity, self-discipline, responsibility, and material well-being." He also shares the modernization theorists' proclivity for parent-child metaphors. Rodney explains the dynamics of dependence:

> When a child or the young of any animal species ceases to be dependent upon its mother for food and protection, it can be said to have developed in the direction of maturity. Dependent nations can never be considered developed. [Independence requires] a capacity to exercise choice in external relations, and above all it requires that a nation's growth at some point must become self-reliant and self-sustaining (1981: 3).

Amin (1974b: 393) also defines "development in the true sense" as "autonomous and self-sustained growth."

Nandy (1983: 120) has noted that childhood innocence served as the prototype of primitive communism in Marx's theory of progress, "which he [Marx] conceptualized as a movement from pre-history to history and from infantile or low-level communism to adult communism." As Melotti (1977: 30) summarizes Marx, in primitive societies "the individual has not yet severed the umbilical cord that unites him to the commune and is still a long way from individualizing himself through the historical process."

It is significant that this powerful metaphor for development has been used by both modernization and dependency theorists. The view of the stages of state and societal development as akin to the stages of human development is rich with assumptions about the helpless state of childhood and the unquestioned need to lessen dependence upon the mother. The metaphor serves to define national dependency as an inability to achieve maturity. Underdevelopment is defined as a *lack:* "lack of heavy industry, inadequate production of food, unscientific agriculture—those are all characteristics of the underdeveloped economies" (Rodney 1981: 18). In such a formulation, underdevelopment is simultaneously linked to both childlike dependence and "primitive" society.

This conception of capitalism emphasizes its progressive characteristics and its steadily expanding control over nature. Rodney (1981: 98), in discussing the disastrous consequences in Africa of slavery, notes that the reduction of population caused Africans to "lose their battle to tame and harness nature—a battle that is at the basis of development." Adopting this conception of capitalist development enables many dependency theorists to sweep away, or render invisible, traditional social relations and practices. But in doing so, oppositions that should be conceived of as dialectical become anchored in the oppositional categories of "productive" and "unproductive" labor. Cardoso (1977: 10) argues that this deterministic inclination "must have something to do with Marxism itself." A feminist-inspired rereading of these texts suggests that the tendency reflects a particular way of thinking about gender, nature, and necessity.

Di Stefano (1991a: 124) suggests that Marx's framework depends on the juxtaposition of necessity and freedom in explaining his view of the unfolding of history and the assertion of control over nature, which celebrates "self-defined and self-created humanity" (Di Stefano 1991a: 127). Activity associated with the realm of necessity characterizes the life of "natural man," whose labor constitutes "mere energy expended to satisfy immediate physical needs and has little in common with human productive activity . . . only man is capable of genuinely creative work" (Ollman 1971: 83). Avineri (1968: 153) notes that Marx saw capitalism as a "highly developed stage in the unfolding of man's creative powers," made possible by the "emergence of civil society, i.e., an autonomous sphere of economic activity, unimpeded by political and religious restrictions" (Avineri 1968: 155). In other words, Marx viewed freedom and the development of capitalism as the movement from "natural" necessity, through the domination of nature and the break with tradition (Mills 1991: 173).

Women are implicated in this orientation toward nature in a variety of ways. First, the domination of nature is conceived of as a primarily male enterprise. Transcending the realm of necessity means to transcend the household through conscious political action in the public sphere (Jaggar 1983: 213). It is the public sphere that allows for the rationalization of human labor and the conscious control and creation of "the products of nature in accord with human needs" (Tucker 1978: 227). In such a conception, women are confined to the private realm of human necessity and family interests.

Second, Marx's conception of labor emphasizes its rational and voluntarist dimensions, as demonstrated by his comparison of the architect and the bee (Tucker 1978: 344–345). The architect purposefully "effects a change in the material on which he works," and imagines a structure "before he erects it in reality." While animals engage in the "mere executions of nature-given instinct" (McMurtry 1978: 22), man is creative and seeks to move beyond the requirements of meeting basic needs. Mary O'Brien (1981: 38) challenges this division of unconscious and conscious labor through her consideration of maternal labor:

> Female reproductive consciousness knows that a child will be born, knows what a child is, and speculates in general about this child's

potential. Yet mother and architect are quite different. The woman cannot realize her visions, cannot make them come true, by virtue of the reproductive labor in which she involuntarily engages, if at all. Unlike the architect, her will does not influence the shape of her product. Unlike the bee, she knows that her product, like herself, will have a history. Like the architect, she knows what she is doing; like the bee, she cannot help what she is doing.

As Di Stefano (1991a: 125–126) notes, Marx's blind spot concerning the link between reproductive and nurturant labor and "productive" labor imposes an economistic and mechanistic construction of humans' awareness of themselves as a species. McMurtry (1978: 52–53) captures this aspect of Marx's thinking in his description of the "new man" who is capable of transcending necessity "by virtue of automated, communist forces of production that provide his material base, his platform of unfettered subjecthood."

▲ The Primacy of Production and Class

These fundamental components of Marx's conceptions of human labor, productive labor, and necessity and freedom are implicitly retained by Latin American dependency theorists such as Cardoso and Faletto (1979). Thus, even while Cardoso (1977) criticizes Frank's deterministic and mechanistic framework, he and Faletto (1979) also render women and gender invisible. *Dependency and Development in Latin America* may be truer to Marx's dialectics, but it retains Marx's blindspot with regard to gender.

The analysis of Cardoso and Faletto is worth discussing at some length because of both its sophisticated approach and its demonstrations of the limits of a dialectical analysis that elides gender. They insist on focusing on "forms of local societies, reactions against imperialism, the political dynamics of local societies, and attempts at alternatives," rather than simply the "logic of capital accumulation" (Cardoso and Faletto 1979: xvi, xv). In place of this logic they propose to view dependency as the "the history of class struggles, of political movements, of the affirmation of ideologies, and of the establishment of forms of domination and reactions to them" (Cardoso and Faletto 1979: xvii). Their book, which covers the various phases of Latin America's relationship to international capital, focuses on the public power struggles between dominant classes and new, nondominant classes that emerge as a result of changes in the conditions of material life. While the analysis is rich in historical detail, its concern nevertheless lies with "the balance of power among social groups" in "their contest for control of the state" (Cardoso and

Faletto 1979: 100, 114). Implicit in this conception of dependency is a portrayal of social classes—the bourgeoisie, landowners, the working class, and the peasant masses—that enter the public arena as rational agents and who achieve agreement on development plans and distributive policies (Cardoso and Faletto 1979: 129–130). While this conception obviously gives priority to class rather than gender, ethnicity, or any other identity, it also represents a Marxist conception of rationality that is expressed in public activity and which in turn is an expression of the dominant mode of production. Rationality is expressed in action, agreements, and pacts consciously arrived at among various classes and the state. This extremely voluntaristic depiction of class struggle omits any consideration of the household. It depicts class struggle as occurring in the public sphere populated by men who seek to alter and challenge conditions of dependency. Women remain isolated in the household and thus are not situated to develop a collective consciousness and lack the capacity for organizing opposition to dependency. Challenging dependency is men's work.

These themes also recur in Samir Amin's work. In *Accumulation on a World Scale* (1974b: 28) he proposes that development be viewed as a series of choices: "shifting the economy's center of gravity" from agriculture to modern industry, industrialization, and "improving the productivity of traditional agriculture." He views the latter task as the most difficult because "social structures, ways of life, and cultures" are bound up with these "primitive techniques." These primitive techniques are not analyzed by Amin because in his framework they are viewed as secondary. Although he (Amin 1974b: 360) suggests a typology of the different types of peripheral capitalist social formations that have emerged in Latin America, the East, and Africa, the underlying explanation for their various configurations lies *outside* of them: "It is through the alliances among classes peculiar to each formation and to the world system that this integration within the unity of the world takes place" (Amin 1977: 190). The determining factor is the mode of production and the problem is the fact that colonial capitalism has blocked the full flowering of industrial development in the periphery. The "social structures, ways of life, and cultures" are not analyzed in any depth; rather, an enlightened revolutionary leadership is called upon to make the correct development choices. In Africa, the only class that shows signs of undertaking development is the rural bourgeoisie:

> In the regions affected by progress, the social upheavals have been radical and fast. Numerous strata of the planters have broken with tradition; they engage in precise calculations and European ways of life and consumption (Amin 1974b: 368).

Such developments, however, were limited to those areas where "structures of the traditional social hierarchies, rural population densities, and access to international migrations" facilitated the emergence of a bourgeoisie (Amin 1990: 110). Thus Amin's analysis reduces national developments to broad structural characteristics that serve the functions of world capitalism. The mode of production mechanistically determines the relations of production, while domestic labor, household production, and the role of women in public production are invisible.

Amin believes that these development choices are the key to national liberation for Third World social formations and that the persistence of primitive agricultural techniques will barely ensure survival. His definition of development, like that of modernization theory, links rural agriculture with primitive tradition and attributes the causes of underdevelopment to insufficient industrialization. Areas outside of capitalist development continue to represent "vestiges of the past," and world capitalism's increasing ability to unify the world has relegated "regional peculiarities to the museum of survivals from the past" (Amin 1974b: 377, 378). Social reform movements with a "traditional appearance" actually "represent ways of surviving in the dramatic conditions of marginality" (Amin 1974a: 25). Only "self assertion" as "complete nations" by those who are "victims of the present set-up" can bring about a socialist world (Amin 1974b: 33). Genuine independence, in Amin's formulation, means escaping the control of one nation by another through the assertion of autonomy.

And, while Amin (1974a: 19) rejects the wholesale adoption of Western technology, he nevertheless maintains that autonomous scientific and technological research in the Third World is necessary for self-reliance. He also argues that modern techniques must be used to improve the condition of the masses: "It is only this immediate improvement . . . which will enable the release of productive enterprise and initiative and the mobilization of the masses in the usual sense of the word" (Amin 1974a: 19).

Like Cardoso and Faletto, Amin gives priority to the mode of production in describing the types of classes that emerge from a given peripheral social formation's encounter with colonial capitalism. The "alliance of foreign capital, state functionaries, and local tribute-receiving classes" (Medley 1989: 89) are the main actors in Amin's model, while the oppressed masses are superexploited through unequal exchange between center and periphery.

Nicholson (1987: 18–19) has noted that Marx moved from a broad to narrow conception of production, largely referring to it as the production of food and objects. The primacy of the economic is

also evident in dependency theory. Cardoso and Faletto (1979) structure their analysis of dependency and underdevelopment around historical periods in which the organization of production plays a central role in shaping local dependence: export-oriented agricultural
growth, the Great Depression, import-substitution industrialization,
and the internationalization of capital are the major periods that
mark the emergence of new modes of dependency. Changes in the
mode of production produce changes in the way in which local and
international classes compete to either deepen or transform the organization of production and consumption (Cardoso and Faletto
1979: 16). They classify countries into those where production is
largely under national control and those where an enclave economy
predominated:

> The beginning of an industrial bourgeoisie with the corresponding
> technically trained professionals, the civil and military bureaucracy,
> the white-collar workers, and so forth depended on the way the ex-
> port system was organized in each country (Cardoso and Faletto
> 1979: 75).

Although they insist that the emergence of social groups was not a
mechanical result of an "economic structure," they often make statements about the congruence between systems of production and
class relations, with the former determining the latter. For example,
they argue that the diversification of the export economy "assumed
different forms according to how diversified production was in each
country, which determined the structural possibilities for action for
the various classes and groups" (Cardoso and Faletto 1979: 102).
They define the "fundamental historical actors" in Latin America as
"classes and groups defined within specific forms of production"
(Cardoso and Faletto 1979: 201).

Amin takes a similar approach in his analysis of underdevelopment in West Africa. Amin (1973: 226) argues that the origins of
change from outward-directed growth to internally generated development will only occur when new "social forces appear, open to the
future rather than dominated by the past, and capable of conceiving
a strategy for liberation that goes beyond the narrow horizons of
minor ex-colonial servants." Like Cardoso and Faletto, Amin posits
a congruence between the mode of production and class structure in
West Africa, while the social forces he describes remain remarkably
flat and mechanical manifestations of these distorted economies.
This reductionism is especially evident in his analysis of Ghanaian
politics under Nkrumah. Ghana had exhausted its export-oriented
growth strategy (centered around cocoa production) years before
and was being pushed toward locally generated development. This

strategy activated the right wing, centered around the landed classes, who consolidated their power by striking alliances with chiefs and intellectuals: "Nkrumah never attempted to fight this opposition by asking for support from agricultural workers, who were still unorganized, or the urban workers, who themselves were victims of inflation" (Amin 1973: 247). The lower classes are depicted as disorganized victims; the propertied classes are depicted as powerful coalition-builders; the household is invisible.

▲ Modes of Production: Where Is the Household?

Frank published *Dependent Accumulation and World Development* (1979) to address critics who argued that his analysis was too focused on external exchange relations to the exclusion of production and ignored the diversity of modes of production in the periphery. But Frank's discussion remains focused on the function of the periphery in the three-phase development of world capitalism (mercantilism, industrialism, and finance capitalism). Political struggles are reduced to analyses of how one class triumphed over the other. In India, for example, the old landlords were "converted into agents of world capitalism" after the British successfully solved the land question in Bengal (Frank 1979: 90). The struggle for independence in midnineteenth century Latin America took place between exporters and manufacturers, and the "export-oriented interests and their metropolitan allies invariably won" (Frank 1979: 85). The process of incorporating the periphery is represented mechanistically and in functionalist terms. World capitalist expansion leads to the

> incorporation—or where necessary the creation—of a local class and its subordinate agents whose economic and political interests are tied to the metropolis, and whose pursuit of economic and political policies in their own self-interest will also serve the metropolis, though it will generate the development and underdevelopment for their country and people (Frank 1979: 146).

Frank repeatedly employs the language of functionalism to explain the mode of production in Asia, Africa, and Latin America (Frank 1979: 17, 43, 149). In Frank's framework all "traditional" or precapitalist social relations are destroyed with the expansion of West European capitalism. The chief struggle is between center and periphery, where at times indigenous capitalism "unsuccessfully struggles" for power against metropolitan capital but ultimately fails. Once again, precapitalist social formations are portrayed as collective victims lacking social agency and as functionalist elements of global capitalism.

Other explorations of the mode of production have produced more nuanced accounts but they too rarely move beyond tracing the way in which the mode of production reproduces itself and interacts with the dominant (capitalist) mode of production. Davidson's (1989: 245) review of the mode-of-production school of dependency outlines the two key assumptions of this approach: the way a society "provides for material needs constitutes the basis for the development of social, political, and ideological forms"; and, the mode of production "characterizes the social organization of men's and women's interactions with nature," thus confirming the continuing primacy of production.

One of the chief concerns of the mode-of-production approach is with the way in which capitalism often coexists with and buttresses precapitalist social formations (Foster-Carter 1978: 51). Phillippe Rey suggests that the "articulation" between the two modes proceeds in three stages: capitalism first reinforces the precapitalist mode; then capitalism takes root, subordinating the precapitalist mode; and finally the precapitalist mode disappears (quoted in Foster-Carter 1978: 56). In interesting language, Rey (as quoted in Foster-Carter 1978: 57) conceptualizes the establishment of capitalist domination as a "combat between the two modes of production, with the confrontations and alliances which such a combat implies: confrontations and alliances between the classes which these modes of production define." Like Cardoso and Faletto's analysis of dependency in Latin America, Reys' approach remained focused on the battles between classes of men in the transformation of one mode of production to another.

Cliffe (1982: 262) attempts to use Reys' framework to analyze the articulation of modes of production in East Africa. In Cliffe's view, Rey "does not lose sight of the specifics of the African experience but situates them within a more global process." Cliffe (1982: 271) describes the structure of the preexisting social formations as taking one of five forms: feudal, tributary, lineage, slave, or pastoral. Colonial capitalism expected different societies to perform certain tasks, but in forcing these tasks upon the African population, the precapitalist modes were first incorporated to serve capitalism rather than being obliterated (Cliffe 1982: 260). The different precapitalist formations combine with the "needs" of capital to produce different class structures with a general tendency toward the emergence of a "kulak-bureaucratic bourgeoisie-international capital pattern as the basis for the neocolonial state in Africa" (Cliffe 1982: 277).

Gibbon and Neocosmos (1985: 158) argue that these "articulationist" views of the precapitalist modes of production replicate the essentialist notion of a peasant economy and produce a "mechanical dualism." The idea that capitalism inevitably produces a hierarchy of domination through its violent undermining of the peasant mode is also not very different from the dichotomous and mechanistic approach of early dependency theorists. Gibbon and Neocosmos (1985: 168) attempt to remedy this with a discussion of the way in which peasant commodity production is not the polar opposite of wage labor but rather "equally the product of capitalist relations." Petty commodity production is carried out by "commodity producers who possess the means of production necessary to produce commodities and who engage in production on the basis of unpaid household labor alone," which in fact is constantly reproduced in Africa (Gibbon and Neocosmos 1985: 170). The state and the ruling class reflect this mode of production and are in constant struggle with local and international classes.

While analyses of the mode of production do provide more detail about class, state, and local politics, they retain dependency theory's tendency to focus on class at the expense of all other struggles. Gibbon and Neocosmos, for example, subsume peasant households and unpaid household labor under the rubric of petty commodity production. Nicholson (1987: 24) notes that the consequence of placing primary emphasis upon class position in relation to the means of production is that historical conflicts "over other socially necessary activities such as childbearing and childrearing" are ignored. As O'Brien (1981: 170) notes, with such a conception, man produces himself and history with a force "mysteriously appropriated from reproductive process." This results in a juxtaposition of a continuously dynamic and changing public realm with an immutable private realm that does not make history nor affect social relations of production.

Furthermore, dependency theory, following Marx, presents a plastic conception of human nature (Di Stefano 1991a: 128). Marx's great accomplishment was to challenge liberalism's model of pre-social individuals and insist that human nature is necessarily constituted in society. His failing, as Heilbroner (1980: 163) notes, is that "we then have a web of social determinations that has no points of anchorage other than our animal bodies." Furthermore, as Di Stefano (1991a: 128) points out, this social construction of the modern subject presupposes the unacknowledged labor of the mother. This reading suggests that a plastic conception of human nature is at least partially rooted in interpretations of gender differences and is produced by male hegemony and power (Chodorow 1989: 111).

▲ Conclusion

Even when dependency theory and mode of production analyses attempt to explore social formations in the periphery, they do so in a way that continues to treat precapitalist modes of production as collective entities lacking historical agency and acted upon by global capitalism. This is largely because capitalism is conceptualized as the dynamic and determining factor of development and underdevelopment in the periphery. Politics in the periphery is conditioned by the types of classes and class alliances that emerge. Other significant attributes of human societies such as gender are subsumed under the politics of production and class formation. Because dependency and mode of production theorists have such unreserved praise for science, technology, and industrialization, which in turn are linked with capitalism, precapitalist social formations tend to be analyzed in a functionalist manner. Precapitalist formations serve the "global logic of capitalism" and they are transformed to serve the needs of capital. For dependency theorists, the goal of revolution should be self-reliant, autonomous development. Embedded in this account is an image of public man at the vanguard of a revolutionary movement that achieves self-sufficiency and transforms the natural world. And, as Thompson (1986: 109) puts it, "the vanguard always seems to be where women are not." Rather, women are assumed to be the exploited and oppressed victims of capitalism. Centuries of capitalist exploitation have left women isolated and trapped within society's most backward institutions. Most women are therefore not fully conscious historical agents. In order to achieve the appropriate level of consciousness, women must engage in public production and adopt the (male) proletarian standpoint. Women are invited into revolutionary politics as the member of a class; other sources of conflict are viewed as subsidiary.

While modernization theorists sought to feminize traditional society and relied upon powerful negative associations between tradition and historic constructions of the feminine, dependency theorists take a more complicated stance with regard to the household. On the one hand, it is implicitly portrayed as stagnant, the site of immutable reproductive activity. On the other hand, some dependency theorists, notably Frank, tend to portray the "unproductive" sectors of society as victims of centuries of capitalist and colonial exploitation. These two strands of dependency theory and the Marxist framework within which it is grounded emerge in formulations of the "woman question" in Southern African revolutions. The analysis of these revolutions demonstrates the masculinist predilections of the dependency/Marxist paradigm in practice; chiefly, the way in which male dominance within the household is accepted as "natural" and the causes of women's subordination are shifted to predatory colonial capitalism. At the same time, women are invited to enjoy the gains of the revolution to the extent they are able, through class position and family ties, to take advantage of civil and political rights conferred in the public sphere.

▲ Implications for Revolutionary Practice

In addition to being deficient in recognizing the household as a site of change and conflict, claims about women's oppression and a focus on production at the expense of reproduction have made many of these revolutionary projects vulnerable to opposition movements. They often implicitly play upon male anxiety about changes that have taken place in gender relations but which are neglected by official formulations. In effect, by officially portraying women as vulnerable and the household as the site of unanalyzed "backward" practices, revolutionary governments have allowed opposition movements such as, in Angola, the Uniao Nacional para a Independencia Total de Angola (National Union for the Total Independence of Angola—UNITA) and, in Mozambique, the Movimento Nacional de Resistencia (MNR) to exploit male anxiety over changes in gender relations. The inherently contradictory way in which these governments approached gender relations has made it easier for opposition movements to base their appeal upon "traditional," rural, and patriarchal ways of life.

▲ Notes

1. I borrowed the term in the subhead (*Masculine Marx*) from Di Stefano's (1991b) aptly titled article about Marx's masculine worldview.

▲ 6
Contradictions in the Challenges to Dependency: The Roots of Counterrevolution in Southern Africa

In the 1970s, it was often argued that the "second wave" of African socialism would usher in an era of genuinely revolutionary politics, especially in countries in Southern Africa where anticolonial guerrilla struggles had taken place. Many Africanists began referring to the newly independent regimes in Angola (1975), Mozambique (1975), and Zimbabwe (1980) as Afro-Marxist or Afro-Communist, to distinguish them from earlier African socialist regimes such as Tanzania, Ghana, and Guinea, and to emphasize the nationalist flavor of their Marxism: eclectic ideologies, flexible organizational structures, and pragmatic leadership (Rosberg and Callaghy 1979; Ottaway and Ottaway 1986; Crawford Young 1984).

In the effort to distinguish Afro-Marxist regimes from their African socialist counterparts, many pointed to the determination to create vanguard parties, the primacy of class struggle, and affinities with the Soviet bloc as significant. An initially overlooked but important aspect of the new revolutions was the conditions they created for debates about women and gender in postcolonial society. In Angola and Mozambique, sites of the revolutions that are the main subject of this chapter, the embrace of Marxism-Leninism and the battle against Portuguese colonial rule put pressure on the male-dominated leadership of the *Movimento Popular de Libertaçao de Angola* (MPLA—the Popular Movement for the Liberation of Angola) and the *Frente de Libertaçao de Mocambique* (Frelimo—Front for the Liberation of Mozambique) to address the "woman question" in the postindependence period.

▲ The Revolutionary Context

Transitions to socialism in the periphery are fraught with obstacles. Weak economies, rudimentary political organizations, and the recent, fragile attainment of political consciousness among workers and peasants are the legacies of oppressive colonial rule. External destabilization has been a feature of virtually every Third World revolution, and devastating wars have been carried out by South African and U.S.-backed counterrevolutionary movements. The nearly twenty-year-old war in Angola has killed nearly 500,000 people, produced 50,000 orphans, and denied approximately 7 million of the country's 10 million people access to clean water (Finkel 1992: 63–64). In Mozambique, an estimated 4 to 5 million people (out of a population of 16 million) have been driven from their homes, and by 1987–1988 nearly half of all primary schools and one-third of the health network had been destroyed (Harsch and Laishley 1993: 3, 13).

Under such conditions, the dynamics of such struggles as those of gender and class in the transition to socialism are assigned to the future: "First defense, then peace, and socialism later" (Vilas 1988: 184–185). The resource expenditure required to defend the revolution explains an obvious impulse to postpone gender and class struggles indefinitely.

Nevertheless, despite continuous destabilization and the death of important leaders (Agostinho Neto in 1979 in Angola and Samora Machel in 1986 in Mozambique) there have been achievements that, along with the setbacks and contradictions, deserve examination. They include attempts to lay the foundations for new forms of democratic participation and establish a new political system that pays more than lip service to egalitarianism. Gender issues have played a role in the forging of new policies partly because the postindependence commitments made to Marxism-Leninism pushed the quest for gender equality even further than the challenge to gender roles that took place during the lengthy guerrilla struggles for liberation. Perhaps as much as modernization theory has endorsed capitalism, dependency theory has been an important framework for viewing the challenges of underdevelopment for revolutionary leaders in the periphery. Themes of dependency theorists are often echoed in revolutionary discourse that emphasizes the need to struggle against imperialism, bourgeois hegemony, and underdevelopment.

▲ Accomplishments of the Revolutions

It would be difficult to overestimate the formidable obstacles faced by Angola and Mozambique after the achievement of independence in 1975. Despite the fact that women had participated in the struggle for national liberation—and had engaged in new political activities, including gender struggles—the large majority of women continued to labor in the rural areas. Although the colonial use of male contract labor and seasonal male employment in diamond mines in Angola and tea and cotton plantations in Mozambique gave some women increased control over household resources, economic opportunities remained limited (Heywood 1987: 370; Isaacman and Stephen 1980: 11).

The revolutions opened up new political opportunities for every Angolan and Mozambican citizen. Campaigns for literacy and healthcare and the initiation of struggles for legal changes by women's organizations are testimony to the accomplishments of governments that were constantly attempting to maintain national sovereignty against South Africa and South African–backed counterrevolutionary groups. In Angola, four women were elected to the important Central Committee; in Mozambique, thousands of women were elected to local people's assemblies in the first-ever elections, held in 1977 (Scott 1986: 123). In Angola, it was reported that 42 percent of the 673,968 people who had become literate in the first eight years of independence were women (OMA 1984: 102). The urban populations of both countries benefited from such government policies as increases in the minimum wage and large subsidies for consumer items (Hanlon 1984: 179).

Through membership drives and regular meetings with party officials, the women's organizations in both countries challenged the party's framing of the issues. In one particularly poignant moment during the women's organization meeting in Mozambique, President Machel's wife won a standing ovation when she said, "Mr. President, we have been forced to keep quiet for 500 years. We only want to speak" (Africa Contemporary Record 1984–1985: 679). The Angolan women's organization frankly noted that "men in our country behave like chiefs with absolute and unlimited powers" (OMA 1984: 62). The revolutions in these two countries undoubtedly brought about the democratization of state power and in the process augmented the powers of some workers, peasants, and women and initially improved the quality of life for many people.

Despite the achievements of these revolutions, the embedded masculinist characteristics of Marxism produced contradictions in state policies, and as state leaders attempted to forge new policies they wound up deferring to male authority in the rural areas, where patriarchal control remains strongest. This also opened up oppositional space for counterrevolutionary movements, which sought support around the reconstitution of "traditional" and "tribal" rural life.

While a major contention of this chapter is that a feminist interrogation of Marxism and dependency sheds light on the nature of counterrevolution in Southern Africa, it is important to keep in mind that the dynamics of counterrevolution obey more than an emphasis on a return to "traditional" constructions of gender relations. Both UNITA in Angola (*Unaio Nacional para a Independencia Total de Angola*—National Union for the Total Independence of Angola) and the MNR in Mozambique (*Movimento Naçional de Resistencia*—National Resistance Movement) presented their counterrevolutionary movements in ethnic and religious terms and as movements struggling against the "new colonizer," the Soviet Union. Furthermore, the postcolonial state structures inherited by the MPLA and Frelimo were remarkably weak and vulnerable to the onslaught of counterrevolutionary movements generously aided by the United States and South Africa. But there has also been a concurrent emphasis upon a defense of "tradition," which itself relies upon constructions of gender roles that attempted to preserve male power in the face of the modernizing ideology of the national regime. Very often, the "foreign" ideology of Marxism-Leninism was portrayed as an attempt to disrupt traditional social relations and, rarely explicitly discussed but implicated nonetheless, gender roles.

▲ Adding "Women as Producers" to Marxist Formulations

Ong (1986: 72) has argued that inadequate conceptualization and theoretical misconceptions have plagued the formulation of gender issues in the revolutions in Southern Africa. In Ong's view, the chief flaws lie with a Marxist approach that ignores women's oppression by men and defines women's work as being "outside the sphere of socially productive work" (Ong 1986: 74). Numerous feminist critics of Marxism have voiced similar claims about the need to augment categories of production and add patriarchal exploitation to our understanding of capitalist exploitation (see, e.g., Bandarage 1984; Molyneux 1986). Kruks and Wisner (1989: 165) suggest that analysis must focus on "women as *producers*, as well as reproducers, and on family relations and the political and planning processes as they affect women as *producers*" (emphasis in original). In this formulation women are elevated alongside men as producers—the politics of production is still given primacy by critics of Marxist-Leninist revolutionary discourse and practice. Many critics of the practice of Third World revolutionary regimes concede the Marxist contention that labor in the public sphere of production is the most important site of struggle: "Production is the one constant, unchanging structure within which human history unfolds and on which the flux of human history depends" (Balbus 1982: 15). Di Stefano (1991b: 158) argues that this "theoretical universe is bound up with an ontological habitat that is profoundly masculine."

Likewise, the masculinist preoccupations of dependency theorists, evident in their emphasis on voluntarism, dichotomies between productive (male) and unproductive (female) labor, and their uncritical praise for the progressive character of ever-widening capitalist exploitation, should make us hesitant to supplement Marxist categories that are so gendered in their understanding of the causes of and solutions to underdevelopment. This also suggests that policies pursued by state and party leaders in Angola and Mozambique are marked by gender at a fundamental level and are not merely inadequate conceptualizations and theoretical misconceptions. A masculinist epistemology is evident in policies embraced by state leaders in the postrevolutionary period and in the way in which the household has been treated by state leaders. On the other hand, revolutionary struggle did create conditions for debates and struggles over gender relations, and state leaders have at times endorsed women's liberation. Ultimately, however, these official commitments to gender equality keep running up against masculinist conceptions about the meaning of modernity and a nationalist impulse to preserve "traditional" male prerogatives within the family.

▲ Public Discourse on Gender and Women

MPLA and Frelimo formulations of the "woman question" depoliticize the household and give precedence to rationalized labor and production, particularly on state farms and cooperatives, and in factories. The First Party Congress of the MPLA emphasized the need to strengthen the worker-peasant alliance, form rural cooperatives, and attain preindependence levels of production (MPLA 1977: 32). While at the First Conference of Mozambican Women (*Organizaçao dos Mulheres de Mocambique*—OMM)in 1973, President Machel rejected arguments for postponing women's liberation until after the revolution (Machel 1981: 21), he also insisted that the chief contradiction was between "women and the private ownership of the means of production," while "the marriage system, marital authority based solely on sex, the frequent brutality of the husband and his consistent refusal to treat his wife as an equal" constituted secondary contradictions (Machel 1981: 24–25). Furthermore, he argued that

> Men and women are products and victims of the exploitative society which has created and formed them. It is essentially against this society that men and women should fight united. Our practical experience has proved that the progress achieved in the liberation of women is the result of the successes gained in our common struggle against colonialism and imperialism (1981: 25).

The 1976 program for action of the OMM emphasized the importance of women's participation in production as a way of eradicating old ideas that inhibited women from participating in "public and social life" (Arnfred 1988: 11). At the Third Party Congress in 1977, Frelimo emphasized that the "battle for production" had replaced the battle for liberation as the newly constituted Marxist-Leninist party's main task (Kruks and Wisner 1989: 151). In 1981, the secretary for ideology of the Central Committee of Frelimo exhorted the OMM to "concentrate its activity on what constitute at this moment the two principal tasks of all citizens . . . the increase of production and productivity" (quoted in Arnfred 1988: 13). The MPLA's First Party Congress also glossed over class differences among women and "secondary contradictions" within the household by arguing that the OMA (*Organizaçao dos Mulheres de Angola*—Organization of Angolan Women) is "an organization of all Angolan women which fights for their emancipation and involvement in the tasks of the revolution" (MPLA 1977: 13).

This emphasis upon winning the battle for production while consigning gender to the realm of secondary contradictions has several important consequences. First and most obviously the division of labor within the household is largely ignored and therefore women's ability to participate in factory and collective farm production is limited. If women remain in charge of agricultural work and maintain responsibility for the children and household then the possibilities for participation in other activities are limited.

Furthermore, in both Angola and Mozambique political participation remained centered around household and family concerns such as vaccination campaigns.[1] While important, such participation reinforces rather than challenges the double burden; and cultural notions about "women's work" are transferred to the public realm.

A second consequence of this emphasis upon public production has been deference to male prerogatives within the household. For example, in 1980 Frelimo published a "family law" that made divorce easier, but Urdang (1989: 204) reports that in interviews conducted with women in the 1980s Frelimo frowned on divorces because "the children won't know their fathers." The Family Law was so controversial that its full adoption was postponed. The MPLA has avoided much public discussion of bride-price and other "feudal practices" because it evoked hostility from "traditionalists" (Wolfers and Bergerol 1983: 126). In this sense, both governments have attempted to maintain political support by conceding the terrain of the household to male authority. This has had the effect of also making women vulnerable in other areas of life. The best example of this vulnerability was Operation Production, carried out in Maputo, Mozambique, in

1983. Operation Production was a program to move the unemployed outside of the capital to rural areas in the north in order to cultivate unutilized farmland. Women were particularly vulnerable to abuses of power by officials who eagerly labeled them unproductive (Urdang 1989: 189). The construction of women as culturally "backward" (discussed below) made it easier for public officials to use bureaucratic power against women.

Another important theme that emerges in public discourse is the depiction of women as passive victims, "doubly oppressed by capitalist society and family tradition" (OMA 1984: 39). In the report of the Central Committee to the First Party Congress of the MPLA, women are defined as "one of the strata of our population who have greatly suffered from the vicissitudes of colonial exploitation and capitalist mentality that dominated our country" (quoted in OMA 1984: 35). According to Kruks and Wisner (1989: 154–155), "Frelimo sees privatization and isolation, leading to general political backwardness, as major effects of both the traditional and the colonial treatment of women." As President Machel (1981: 24) noted, "all superstitions and religions find their most fertile soil among women, because they are immersed in the greatest ignorance and obscurantism." The president also noted, however, in the year following independence, that "the first essential task is to destroy the colonialist structures and the capitalist structures" in the country (Munslow 1985: 172), thus giving cultural practices deemed backward and traditional lower priority.

Presenting women as an "extreme and telling example of the marginalization of the periphery" (Jaquette 1982: 273) is a classic formulation used by dependency theorists to analyze the victims of capitalist exploitation. In the context of revolutionary politics in Southern Africa, the chief consequence of this formulation is that it renders the household unworthy of analysis because it is the site of immutable, traditional, and ignorant cultural practices and social relations. The site of oppression is shifted from the household to colonial public policies and the abstract force of capitalism that have left women powerless victims. This "doubly oppressed" approach to the analysis of gender makes discussion of male domination within the household theoretically and practically off-limits. It implies that the only approach to women's liberation is through their participation in the public sphere, which has been revolutionized by an enlightened male leadership.

This portrayal of women as victims also helps validate the party's definition of the meaning of modernity and development, one that uncritically accepts the liberating potential of advanced technology, heavy industry, and bureaucratic rationalization. Both Frelimo and the MPLA devoted the bulk of investment to state farms in the postindependence period, while rural cooperative and peasant associations (precursors to fully constituted cooperatives in Angola) received very little funding. Tensions between centralization and decentralization within the vanguard party have frequently been resolved in favor of centralization, thus limiting the ability of the women's organizations to affect party policy and ensuring that the leadership plays the most powerful role in shaping development issues. Emphasizing hierarchy, production, and advanced technology reinforces the tendency to devalue women's contributions to production and creates a stark contrast between modern technology and constructions of women as backward and traditional. The construction of modernity and tradition as polar opposites thus inextricably links women with tradition, ignorance, and backwardness.

This is also evident in the consistent tendency to define the household as a drag on women's ability to participate in the tasks of national reconstruction. Although the household division of labor is recognized as a "fundamental problem" by the OMA (1984: 42), there is no discussion of the way in which male domination ensures the double burden, and no recognition of the inevitable male resistance that would accompany full-fledged attempts to collectivize child-care and agricultural production. Ong (1986: 85) notes this contradictory approach in the OMA discussion of fertility and motherhood: while it was argued that women should have the right to freely consented motherhood, men's power in imposing their sexuality upon women is not discussed. The congress's injunction to wage a struggle against underdevelopment rather than male dominance precludes a full treatment of the division of labor within the household and presents the two issues as mutually exclusive rather than connected. The inherent limitation of Frelimo's policy is demonstrated by its exhortations about women's involvement in production while at the same time insisting that women are responsible for the younger generation because of "the place they occupy in the family structure" (Frelimo 1983: 138). As Kruks and Wisner (1984: 115) point out, the aim of the party was to involve women "*qua* mothers and educators in the wider process of social emancipation from which they too were to benefit." The focus on production meant that the gender struggles that took place during the colonial wars were no longer viewed as an integral part of general societal transformation. Along with the reassertion of male power in northern Mozambique, Arnfred (1988: 8–9) witnessed the resurgence of initiation rites as an effort on the part of women in Cabo Delgado Province to assert a "collective female gender identity." Urdang (1989: 215) discovered that some women supported the continuation of *lobolo* [brideprice] as a way of strengthening marriage and protecting against abuse and desertion. For many women, "the past is not simply one of 'oppression' nor is the future an obvious 'progression'" (Arnfred 1988: 9). Practices that the parties would officially designate as "feudal" are tightly bound up with material conditions. Exhorting women to combat these practices while simultaneously ignoring both their gendered and material foundations means that the parties have conceded an important arena of contestation in postrevolutionary society.

These party pronouncements reflect ambiguities and contradictions that arise as a result of palpably masculine theorizing about the public and private spheres, which goes beyond problems of the Marxist-Leninist position (i.e., that the transformation of the social relations of production will necessarily produce changes in household relations and the relations of reproduction). Party pronouncements also reflect an inability to address or even analyze the contradictions and struggles within the household. OMA, presumably as a result of the pressures from the male-dominated MPLA, has avoided open opposition to bride-price because it would evoke hostility from "traditionalists" (Wolfers and Bergerol 1983: 126). In addition, bride-price and other practices such as polygamy are characterized as "feudal practices" by both parties, which has the effect of equating such practices with dehistoricized "tradition" rather than inextricably bound up with social organization and the relations of production. Kruks and Wisner (1984: 120) make this same point in their criticism of treating such practices as simply relics from a distant past that oppress women: "Polygamy is not simply a 'social problem of women': it is also a relation of production."

Party formulations are aimed at the male individual abstracted from "superstition and obscurantism" and oriented toward an autonomous identity unencumbered by the "privatized and irrational" desires of the household (Elshtain 1981: 119). What is striking is the extent to which the discourse of the revolutionary Marxist-Leninist state resembles that of the liberal state. The fundamental feature of this discourse is its dependence upon constructions that buttress "the interests of individual men against the *mandatory* relational situation of women situated in sequestered domains of caretaking" (Brown 1992: 20). This formulation suggests that defending masculine powers and prerogatives depends on the maintenance of distinctions between the public and private spheres. The defense of masculine prerogatives, however, often conflicts with the revolutionary imperative to broaden the public sphere to include women. Depicting the household as backward, private, and isolated while the public arena is occupied by rational classes (of men) whose composition reflects the level of development of productive forces has had political consequences in both countries. The support of the opposition movements in Angola and Mozambique should be viewed in the context of increasing tension and conflict within the household and over women's status. In essence, the limited gains made by women in public life as a result of their participation in the revolution, and state policies in the postindependence period combined with masculinist underanalysis of the household, have created a space in which UNITA and the MNR have moved to call for the reinvigoration of "traditional" institutions and the reinstitution of "appropriate" gender roles.

▲ Backlash in the Countryside

UNITA has undoubtedly served the external interests (of the United States and pre-1994 South Africa) and has reflected fears of ethnic dominance on the part of the Ovimbundu, a major ethnic group in the south-central portion of Angola. Perhaps more importantly, it has increasingly moved away from its Maoist ideology toward efforts to reconstruct Ovimbundu "traditional" institutions and an African nationalist ideology with distinctively conservative tendencies. Jonas Savimbi, the leader of UNITA, has always insisted on respecting the traditions of the peasantry, and he has assiduously cultivated the persona of a "traditional" and "tribal" leader. For example, his name among some Ovimbundu is *Sekulu da Paz*—Elder of Peace (Heywood 1989: 57). In 1979 Savimbi noted:

> My own doctrine is this: why don't we go back to our African roots and analyze them? It is true that we have to work for progress, and in modern times we cannot apply all our traditions without changing them or adjusting them, but we have to keep an *essence* of our values in order to remain a people with an identity (Bridgland 1986: 290).

Savimbi's rhetoric essentializes a unique Angolan tradition revolving around the peasantry and male elder "tribal" authority. The implicit juxtaposition is between tradition and the modernizing and Soviet-inspired ("foreign") ideology of Marxism-Leninism. In an interview with newspaperman Leon Dash, an Angolan UNITA lieutenant-colonel (Dash 1977b: A8) argued that he fought to remove all foreigners from his country because "they want to end our way of life. We will lose our heritage."

Savimbi and UNITA were often portrayed in heroic terms by sympathetic Western journalists, which contributed to the praise of heroic UNITA resistance in the modernizing discourse of Marxism-Leninism.

In 1977, Dash, a *Washington Post* reporter, spent seven-and-a-half months with UNITA guerrillas and carried out several interviews with Savimbi and high-ranking members of his command. Dash (1977a: A24) argued that UNITA's success should be attributed to its "ability to meld strong tribal traditions with their modern-day struggle." Richard Harwood (1981b: A15), a *Washington Post* managing editor, noted the boost in morale provided by rallies that married "traditional African rituals with UNITA's ideological goals." Dash (1977a: A24) quoted Savimbi, who argued that although tribalism is divisive it is "the lifeblood of Africa," thus defending the movement's deferential treatment of chiefs and elders of non-Ovimbundu "tribes" to win them to UNITA's cause. Dash (1977b: A8) argued that it was affinity for tradition, "an emotional attachment to kinship, tribe, and the Angolan south," rather than ideology or South African support, that kept the opposition (UNITA) guerrillas fighting. Savimbi and the UNITA leadership believed that the basic structure of Ovimbundu villages could be used as a model of development in the south-central region of the country, and that Ovimbundu representatives could effectively adapt the structure to non-Ovimbundu areas (Heywood 1989: 60–61).

UNITA ideology also reflects an implicit concern with gender relations and attempts to tap into sentimental and romantic notions of African "tribal" life and women's role within it. In an appeal to village elders, UNITA's secretary-general, Miguel Puna, argued that "the MPLA has been teaching children not to respect their parents" (Bridgland 1986: 365). Bridgland recorded murmurs of approval from villagers and rumbles of approval from "the old men when he [Puna] said he would later hold a meeting restricted to village elders." At UNITA's Fourth Congress in March 1977, the UNITA-controlled territory was declared the Black African and Socialist Republic of Angola in order to reinforce African traditions and build opposition to the "*dirigiste* and anti-religious trends within the MPLA" (Bridgland 1986: 68).

Although there were some female and children guerrillas, their roles, from Dash's account, remained largely associated with the "traditional" female work of preparing food and celebrating military victories. Harwood (1981a: A8) reported on all-male battalions. Dash (1977c: A24) also reported that a UNITA captain, a member of the Ganguela ethnic group of southeast Angola, was reluctant to sit in judgment on a case where two women were accused of witchcraft. He wound up releasing the women, but instructed their accusers to defer to the local chief in such matters, thus abdicating any responsibility for challenging prevailing cultural practices and sanctioning continued male authority over women and persecution of them. In

1983, UNITA's minister of justice, Smart Chata, told Bridgland (1986: 4133) that UNITA's policy was to "encourage people to maintain their culture . . . we incorporate that culture into our political structures."

In Mozambique, the MNR was originally organized and funded by the Rhodesian Central Intelligence Organization, later by South Africa. Similar to UNITA, the MNR is also hierarchically organized, authoritarian, and relies upon forced recruitment. Nevertheless, a number of observers have argued that the MNR's strength in the countryside has increased despite declines in external funding. Clarence-Smith (1989: 9) compares the "Black racism" of the MNR with UNITA because both movements attempt to exploit resentment against whites, *mesticos*, and Indians in the upper echelons of the party-state. In so doing, the MNR, like UNITA, has constructed its limited program around the preservation of tradition and traditional prerogatives. Morgan (1990: 613) argues that Frelimo's opposition to religion, polygamy, and chiefs, officially portrayed as backward institutions and practices, has been met with resistance, particularly in the rural areas. The MNR has attempted to appropriate "both religious symbols and age old customs" including the use of spirit-mediums, in an effort to engender support in the countryside among Shona-speakers in central Mozambique (Morgan 1990: 613). Tom Young (1989: 501) quotes from an interview with MNR Secretary-General Evo Fernandes, who emphasized the deference given to traditional chiefs:

> We are based on the traditional system: the administrative system depends on the area the chieftain has. . . . What happens if the military unit needs new bases? We ask the chieftains where we can settle a base in their area.

Urdang (1983: 27) notes that Frelimo's most successful efforts to eradicate polygamy have occurred in communal villages, which undoubtedly poses a threat to lineage elder dominance. Hall (1990: 56–57) describes the way in which chiefs in northern Cabo Delgado Province invited MNR forces into the region in order to destroy a local communal village and send the people to live in dispersed settlements. Thus, as in Angola, increasing support for the opposition movement should be linked to losses of masculine privilege.

This "traditional" base of resistance also helps explain Frelimo's growing recognition of the power of traditional authorities and the need to defer to them. The party's response has been to suggest that a compromise be struck between the state and local male power. In 1988, Justice Minister Honwana noted:

We are obviously going to have to harmonize traditional beliefs with our political project. Otherwise, we are going against things that the vast majority of our people believe; we will be like foreigners in our own country. . . . We will have to restore some of the traditional structures that at the beginning of our independence we simply smashed, thinking that we were doing a good and important thing (quoted in Young 1989: 507).

▲ The Standpoint of the Male Proletariat

While the exigencies of war, settler flight, and externally backed destabilization created pressures to increase production and central-ization of power in both Angola and Mozambique, the revolutionary discourse of the MPLA and Frelimo resonates with many of the themes present in Marxist-derived dependency theory, discussed in Chapter 5.

At the opening speech of the OMM conference in 1973, Machel characterized women as "the most oppressed, humiliated, and ex-ploited beings in society" (Machel 1981: 20). Colonialism and capi-talism have kept women in "ignorance, obscurantism, and supersti-tion" (Machel 1981: 24). In this view, it is only through women's engagement in production beyond the household that will "release productive forces and launch a process of economic development es-sential to a deeper ideological understanding and sound knowledge of the world around them" (Urdang 1985: 352). Only participation in production *outside* of the household will provide women with the appropriate vantage point for understanding the tasks of the Mozam-bican revolution. In such a formulation, the standpoint of the male proletariat is the privileged position and women must move beyond the household in order to achieve this privileged understanding. It is only through participation in public production that women can contribute to the building of the peasant-worker alliance that pushes the revolution forward.

The link between women, the family, and precapitalist structures is also evident in these formulations. Alternating with the depiction of women as victims who can only achieve liberation through "con-scious political commitment to the revolution" (Urdang 1985: 352) is a vision of the household as a hindrance to the realization of revolu-tionary goals: increased industrialization, production, and self-re-liance. This view of the household is captured in an interesting way in Ake's (1985: 23) discussion of the constraints on the development of proletarian consciousness in Nigeria. It is applicable, in Ake's con-tention, to other African states:

> This problem [constraints on the development of proletarian consciousness] refers to the fact that the proletariat has to have one foot in rural society in order to survive; he invariably has to keep a home in the village, his wife and, most importantly a small farm worked by his wife but with his own intermittent assistance during weekends and leave periods. [This means] that the worker does not fully face the realities of his existence. It inculcates peasant consciousness and tends to impair the worker's ability to struggle.

The household serves as a drag on male ability to recognize the most important struggle he faces. Conversely, the revolutionary potential of women is measured in terms of the extent to which they can contribute to the realm of planned, rational, organized production, which is defined in terms of ever-increasing industrial growth and mechanization. The revolutionary transformation of women becomes defined in terms of equal access to the fruits of revolutionary labor, as in the statement prepared for a 1976 OMM conference:

> The Mozambican peasant woman has to be assured equal opportunities to learn new techniques, to have access to the use of machines, to the acquisition of theoretical knowledge and above all to participation in the political organs, in the direction and management to the same extent as her participation in the work (quoted in Urdang 1985: 363).

This view renders the "obscurantist and superstitious" practices associated with the household superfluous or a mere reflection of the low level of material development of the country. As such, the household is depoliticized and by default made immutably traditional. Thus the larger binary opposition of center-periphery is repeated in these national revolutions: the peripheral household must be modernized through the engine of change, the center-industrial economy.

Finally, the revolutionary leadership of the MPLA and Frelimo, like dependency theorists, envision development as the successful application of science, technology, and planning to the low level of material development of the country. Both leaderships emphasized that the battle of production must take place through industrial development and poured money into mechanized state farms rather than communal or family production (Munslow 1984). The chief struggle is thus between men and nature and between classes of men: an alliance between (male) industrial workers and (male) peasants must be forged to win the battle for production. It is not simply that women's labor is not included in this formulation, which implies that it could easily be added to a revolutionary strategy of transformation. In fact, the realm of women/nature/precapitalism is what must be overcome through revolutionary politics. The "battle for production" slogan implicitly captures a relationship and opposition between heroic male leadership and female passivity within a realm that does not make history. Revolutionary rhetoric exhorts women to make history through a revolutionary commitment to "greater freedom, creativity, self-discipline, responsibility, and material well-being" (Rodney 1981: 3) in the public realm.

▲ Conclusion

Whitehead (1990: 58) has argued that struggles over the control of resources, the growing number of poor female-headed households, urban-rural migration, and war have produced a virtual "sex war" throughout the African continent. Despite official commitments to involving women in the public sphere, revolutionary parties in Angola and Mozambique neglected the persistence of male dominance in the household or depicted women as victims of abstract "feudal practices." This neglect has the effect of juxtaposing the distant past of precolonial tradition within which women labored, with the modernizing present and progressive government.

For both the ruling parties and opposition movements, the household has been contested terrain. For modernizing Marxist-Leninists, the household is officially backward, doubly oppressed by colonialism and capitalism. For "traditionalists," it becomes implicitly bound up with masculinist conceptions of utopian "tribal" life. Male heroic accomplishments and deference to male village elders are key components in the refashioning of a counterdiscourse on African liberation. UNITA and MNR efforts to glorify "traditional" constructions of African life demonstrate the dangers inherent in reviving traditions based on the "complementary" roles of men and women. Official Marxism's successes in affirmative action for women in the public sphere need to be accompanied by a rethinking of the concept of human labor, reproduction, and the contradictory and changing dynamic within the household.

▲ Notes

1. Women have also been involved in literacy campaigns, which while less explicitly linked to the household still assumes that women are responsible for caring duties and educating household members. In Angola, for example, 1979 was declared the Year of the Child to coincide with the U.N. program, and women were given primary responsibility for associated activities. Party decisions to focus literacy campaigns on the workplace excluded many women.

▲ 7
Rethinking Gender and Development

A recent textbook on African politics provided an overview of post–1945 theorizing about development and reiterated the growing consensus that modernization and dependency theory should both be faulted for their failure to capture "many of the significant processes taking place on the continent. . . . Its adherents' grasp of African realities was as skewed, albeit for very different reasons, as that of the modernization writers whom they treated with such contempt" (Chazan et al. 1992: 19). The authors of the textbook advocate a statist approach, defined as a framework that focuses on state-society relationships and examines each side of the relationship with equal thoroughness. Later in the text the authors discuss the "high" politics of state-making and rulemaking practices such as leadership, coalitions, and patronage. They also discuss the "deep" politics of "political conflict that have direct bearing on policy decisions and the dynamics of civil order and disorder in African countries" (Chazan et al. 1992: 189). Deep politics includes elite, factional, communal, mass, and popular conflicts. The authors' description of what counts as politics is both broader than many standard accounts yet narrow in its focus on the public activity of groups and individuals engaged in politics, defined as a "set of transactions, the manifestation of the exercise of choice by multiple actors within existing parameters" (Chazan et al. 1992: 23). The text includes sections on women's organizations and "women's issues"—e.g., education and women's role in the economy. There is no analysis of gender conflicts, no effort to account for the role of the state in reproducing the gendered division of labor, and no discussion of the effects of bureaucratization on women's lives. The text is typical of approaches that seek to go beyond modernization and dependency theory but in fact retain many of the fundamental assumptions contained within those approaches about what counts as politics. Adding women to the new approaches does not alter the basic framework. This study has been about how these basic frameworks are anchored in an often invisible acceptance of binary and gendered oppositions about the meaning of modern politics and the meaning of tradition.

▲ The Benefits of Rereading

One of the most obvious gains from rereading modernization theory is to discover the extent to which Third World women literally served as a point of contrast between meanings of modernity and tradition. Inkeles and Smith, McClelland, and Lerner explicitly contrast the moral conservatism and victimization of women in Third World so- cieties with the liberated women of the West who live in egalitarian relations with their male counterparts. De Groot's (1991: 117) sum- mary of European colonial representations of non-Western women demonstrates the continuity between nineteenth-century European constructions and those of modernization theorists:

> Both non-Westerners and women . . . were understood and repre- sented as less than adult through images and theories about their "child-like," "underdeveloped" character; their status as rational be- ings was denied through emphasis on their "emotional," "unrea- sonable," "instinctive," qualities and behavior. . . . Adulthood and rationality were simultaneously equated with elite, white, male ex- perience and outlook, thus ensuring that women and non-whites alike appeared as both different ("other") *and* inferior, to be un- derstood in terms of their "failure" to attain or "incapacity" for such an experience and outlook.

Development theorists have much to learn from rereading modern- ization theory's depiction of non-Western women as the chief bear- ers of tradition. Mohanty (1991b: 72–73) has explored recent femi- nist scholarship on Third World women and finds that they are often still treated as a uniformly oppressed group because they are "third world women," who "by definition" are religious, family-oriented, conservative, illiterate, and domestic. As long as Third World women are defined as other and peripheral, then "Western Man/Humanism can represent him/itself as the center" (Mohanty 1991b: 73). My ex- plorations have gone beyond an analysis of the explicit representa- tions of women in modernization theory texts to argue that depic- tions of tradition in general are marked by social constructions of gender differences. The texts have been reread for the invested meanings modernization authors have given tradition, many of which center around traits that have been historically associated with women and women's work.

Although dependency theorists recognize the dominance of the West in the world system and the legacy of Western colonialism and imperialism, rereading dependency theory can also be useful. Despite the fact that women are also usually invisible in dependency texts, they are implicitly treated as victims who can only escape this status through class struggle and revolutionary politics. Dependency theory assumes that descriptions of global capitalist development are sufficient for understanding the victim status of peoples (and women) of the Third World. Rereading dependency theory helps us understand what has been left out of these structural accounts of underdevelopment. Dependency theory's account of Third World politics is richer than that of modernization theory yet still only a partial account because it, too, rests on dichotomies that posit essentialized gender differences.

At another level, rereading can contribute to a reconsideration of the way we think about modernity, industrialization, and work. In both modernization and dependency theory, modernity is associated with formal political life in an urban milieu. Hyden's calls for breaking the backbone of the economy of affection could be viewed as a call to discipline or destroy local cultures. Yet Third World industrialization has created disasters such as Bhopal, and even a supposed miracle of development such as the Green Revolution has displaced populations and created hunger and food shortages. Rereading can contribute to the growing movement that seeks to reconsider the meaning of development. Edwards (1989: 120–121) describes these efforts as an attempt to move from treating people as objects to subjects, from objective research to subjective understanding, and from scientific and technocratic expertise to popular and local knowledge. Certain kinds of work—work that, historically, has been done by men—has also been viewed as modern and superior to work done by women. Esther Boserup's (1970: 56) pathbreaking work on the effects of colonialism on women's status, in which she explores, for example, how extension workers favored men and how colonial officials created a division of labor between men and women in growing cash and food crops, wrote this about work:

> It is the men who do the modern things. They handle industrial inputs while women perform the degrading manual jobs; men often have the task of spreading fertilizer in the fields, while women spread manure; men ride the bicycle and drive the lorry while women carry headloads, as did their grandmothers. In short, men represent modern farming in the village, women represent the old drudgery.

While Boserup provides insights into the effects of colonialism on women's status, she also accepts prevailing evaluations attached to the work that men and women do.

Shiva (1990: 191) remarks that associations between modernity, industrialization, and work are embedded in the dualistic thinking inherent in Western patriarchy's project of "development" in the Third World. This project assumes that "nature is unproductive. Organic agriculture based on nature's cycle of renewability is unproductive. Women and tribal and peasant societies embedded in nature are also unproductive." "Female-sphere" theories lead to reevaluations of the domestic sphere and question male definitions of power and development (Jaquette 1982: 280–281). They also come very close to embracing as "natural" the very oppositions that this study has tried to challenge. Female-sphere theories propose an alternative to development that seeks to displace the male subject of development theory. This shift is unlikely to be successful because this strategy replicates the oppositional categories that feminist theory tries to challenge. Female-sphere theory is also grounded in a confidence about a definitive rendering of women's experience that is insufficiently attentive to differences among women. It assumes that "woman" is a knowing subject, and the efforts to "theorize such a subject invariably produces normalizing or essentialist accounts of womanhood which obscure, silence, and misrepresent a great number of women" (Di Stefano 1991a: 192). In short, female-sphere theory is grounded too much in the very practices it seeks to displace and has not provided a way of disaggregating women's experience in a theoretically meaningful way.

On the other hand, the practice of rereading can avoid embracing and glorifying the opposite concept in the gendered pairings of male/female, culture/nature, and modern/traditional and can continue to raise questions about what it means to be modern, what counts as politics, the benefits of industrialization, and valuations of work. Rereading can also provide an opportunity for further criticism of the two prevailing paradigms in development studies and provide a new basis for evaluating the claims of each.

▲ Modernization Theory

The liberal underpinnings of modernization theory are based on a distinction between public and private that excludes the traditional household from public politics. Tradition and the private sphere in fact represent the opposition upon which modernization theorists build their theory of what it means to be modern. Characterizations of traditional communities as parochial, conservative, religious, and suspicious of change are used to demonstrate the benefits of modernity. A few modernization theorists explicitly link tradition with women, tangible evidence that the struggle for modernization is conceived as a struggle against the household. These characterizations ultimately place traditional societies outside of history. Men make history in the rational world of modern politics while women continue their primary "natural" responsibilities within the household.

The abstract individualism of modernization theory conceives of men—usually entrepreneurs—outside and independent of social contexts and interpersonal relations. The definition of modern man given by Inkeles and Smith (1974: 290) captures the essentially abstract individualism of modernization theory. The modern man is

> an informed participant citizen; he is marked by a sense of personal efficacy; he is highly independent and autonomous in his relations to traditional sources of influence, especially when he is making basic decisions about how to conduct his personal affairs; and he is ready for new ideas and experiences, that is, he is relatively open-minded and cognitively flexible.

Modernization theory's concern with self-sufficiency and autonomy joins with assumptions about the importance of entrepreneurship to create a vision of modernity that excludes women, and perhaps depends on the exclusion of women. In providing a description of modernity that juxtaposes acquisitive and innovative man (a "risk taker" to use McClelland's term) with stagnant tradition, modernization theory leaves us with a powerfully masculine view of what it means to be modern.

Perhaps this explains why soft-state and related theories of the ineffectual and patrimonial African state have been reconstituted with such success. Under the guise of proposing a theory about the uniqueness of Africa, soft-state theories bring forth a powerful paradigm that reproduces the gendered oppositions of modernization theory. While the female-headed household provides support and sustenance to communities of family and kin networks (see Hyden 1983b: 11), this same component of the "traditional" community is presented as the obstacle to the achievement of modernity. Tradition and the economy of affection are positioned against the modern state. State authority is naturalized as a universalistic and integrationist force that has the "right" to subvert the autonomy of local communities in the name of a higher authority considered to be more "modern."

▲ Dependency Theory

The strength and brilliance of dependency theory is its attention to the international context of development and the role of power and domination in perpetuating underdevelopment. The global spread of capitalism has impinged directly upon peripheral societies, affecting patterns of accumulation, class structures and alliances, and ideologies. Dependency theory also asks important questions about "how general trends of capitalist expansion turn into concrete relations among men, classes, and the state in the periphery," thus emphasizing the importance of dialectical analysis of the relationship between global capitalism and local structures (Cardoso and Faletto 1979: x). Dependency theory's efforts to analyze concrete situations of dependence also highlight the unilinear and ahistorical aspects of modernization theory.

The discourse of dependency theory, however, displays a tendency to view social formations in the periphery as undeveloped before contact with global capitalism and underdeveloped after being aggressively and rapaciously undermined by colonial and imperial rule. Underdeveloped societies are underanalyzed. Their chief characteristic is their inability to carry out sustained, autonomous growth. Although most dependency theorists argue that global capitalism constitutes the major obstacle to development, there is also a tendency to present Third World social formations as "backward" obstacles in their own right. In addition, subordinated classes of men are portrayed as having lost their autonomy to make the unencumbered development choices. Rodney even compares dependence to childhood and defines self-reliant development as the goal of revolutionary politics.

The primacy of production and class struggle thus anchor dependency theory. Even the modes-of-production approach describes capitalist expansion in terms of how local structures were transformed to serve the needs of capital, primarily through the creation of local classes that serve as agents of international capital (the "comprador" or "bureaucratic" bourgeoisie). The approach ultimately subsumes all conflicts under the rubric of struggles over production. The household is usually invisible in dependency theory but its implicit role is given a particular place in revolutionary theory.

By implication, the household is the last link in Frank's powerful rendering of the metropolis-satellite hierarchy of domination and exploitation. The inhabitants of the household, in revolutionary practice, must engage in production in order to develop genuine consciousness about the significance of class struggle. In fact the revolution promises to usher in material bounty through the application of technology and accomplished by Frank's new generation of scientists in the Third World. As a first step toward rethinking the meaning of development and rewriting development theory, the role of the state and the possibilities of standpoint theory are potentially fruitful areas for analysis.

▲ Prospects for Rewriting: States and Standpoints

Rereading development theory allows us to place it in the larger context of the crisis affecting Western social theory. The theoretical frame of reference employed by both modernization and dependency theorists raises important questions about the subjects of theory, the dichotomies upon which our notions of tradition and modernity rest, and the role of theory in maintaining the essentialist categories that make First World dominance possible. Despite the obvious and important differences in epistemologies and political interests of liberal modernization theory and Marxist-inspired dependency theory, both ground their authority in philosophical understandings of tradition/modernity and precapitalism/capitalism that are distinctly masculinist. Object relations theory, conceptions of the public/private, and renderings of development challenges in terms of triumphalist struggles to overcome feminized tradition, are useful frames of reference for understanding the power of gendered categories in constructing a traditional and modern world. There are also important questions about whether modernization theory and dependency theory should be compared in terms of the extent to which they offer an intelligible account of development and underdevelopment.

Modernization theory's grounding in liberal individualism, its portrayals of individuals as modern men, and its justification of U.S. political power and national security interests demonstrates the relationship between knowledge and power in the creation of development theory and bases its authority on the creation of the Third World as *other.* Dependency theory provides an important critique of development theory and demonstrates the hierarchical way in which the world system is structured. Its critique exposes the way in which liberal modernization theory depends upon and helps construct a Third World that produces exploitation and a division of labor that systematically works to ensure "the construction, regulation, and support of a world system where multinational corporations trade and move capital without restriction from national states" (Harris 1989: 21). Despite dependency theory's tendency mechanistically to propose the liberation of the Third World through an explosion of class consciousness and its flattened view of the household, it still offers a powerful analysis of capital accumulation and the way in which exploitative relations work between core and periphery.

One of the most important insights of dependency theory is its materialist account of the expansion and transformation of capitalism. The state, as a "condensation of class domination" (Ake 1985: 1) plays a crucial role in mediating class struggle between domestic and international capital and is an important site of class formation and class struggle. Unlike Hyden's account of the ineffectual and soft state, a materialist account focuses on the central role of the state in shaping politics, "picking winners," and affecting gender politics.

Characterizations of the postcolonial state have ranged from instrumentalist models that posit a state controlled by the bourgeoisie to ones that emphasize the relative autonomy of the state and the revolutionary potential of postcolonial ruling classes.[1] A second and related approach has been one that concerns itself with defining the class character of the postcolonial state and the nature of the ruling class. There have been efforts to gauge the revolutionary potential of the petty bourgeoisie as well as portrayals of the class struggle between various factions of the petty bourgeoisie (Saul 1979; Currie and Ray 1984).

Fatton's (1988; 1989a; 1989b) materialist account of the African state is an important effort in understanding the nature of the contemporary postcolonial state. Fatton (1988: 255) argues that the African ruling classes are attempting to establish their hegemony through control of the state: "In Africa, class power is state power: the two are fused and inseparable" (Fatton 1988: 254). The relative absence of an indigenous bourgeoisie means that state power offers the best opportunity for consolidating ruling class hegemony. Fatton (1989a: 176) argues against Hyden's portrayal of the soft state; instead, he describes the state as "hard" because the dominant class has yet to become hegemonic. Hegemony is elusive because the ruling classes have yet to convince the "subaltern classes" that their subordination to the dominant classes is inevitable and just—hence the incipient ruling class frequently resorts to authoritarian coercion in order to ensure compliance (Fatton 1989a: 174).

Fatton (1989b) has attempted to include gender in his analysis of the unsteady state and ascending ruling classes in Africa. However, he winds up reducing gender struggle to a component of ruling class efforts to establish hegemony. The ruling classes "have marginalized women and used them as scapegoats for masking failures" (Fatton 1989b: 60). In Fatton's account, ruling-class efforts to portray women as sources of economic competition has "eroded the solidarity of the oppressed" (Fatton 1989b: 60). Gender is a secondary contradiction and functions as an instrument of ruling-class efforts to establish hegemony.

While it is important to provide materialist accounts of the state's role in reproducing gender relations, rereading modernization (and soft-state) and dependency theory has suggested that representations of women and women's lives are as significant as materialist accounts of partially autonomous states that serve as an arena for ruling-class projects and class struggles. Leaders of revolutionary states have created definitions of women's roles in revolutions, and international donors have created definitions of women's roles in capitalist development. Analysis of state practices in the light of these definitions has pointed to important ways in which public discourse constructs the "woman question" and "women's role in economic development." For example, the constructions of women as "doubly oppressed" in Frelimo and MPLA rhetoric is an important means of understanding state policies with regard to women in the economy. The World Bank's shifting representation of women from one that virtually ignored the category in 1981 to a strategy that attempts to incorporate women into structural adjustment programs (by representing women as targets of state policy and as a safety net during the deepening of capitalist development) are also significant. This suggests that categories of representation are as important as materialist accounts in understanding the dynamics of the postcolonial state. Notions of citizenship, politics, and gender relations are revealed through analysis of how state leaders and international capital frame issues of revolution and production. The examination of the interaction between class, gender, and state suggests that each reinforces and gives meaning to the other, in equally important ways. Rather than insisting on the primacy of class politics, this approach gives equal importance to the ways in which the category of "woman" is given content and meaning.

Furthermore, as rereading Hyden particularly demonstrated, representations of gender in academic scholarship play a signficant role in shaping theory. Development theory, especially modernization and soft-state theory, uses gendered categories to define modernity. Mohanty (1991a: 32) remarks on the continuity of colonial strategies of control that relied on racialized and sexualized definitions of "natives" to "consolidate particular relations of rule"; she also emphasizes the continuing role that academic scholarship plays in producing definitions of the so-called Third World. The rereading in this study has demonstrated a powerful continuity between modernization theory and theories of the African soft state and suggests that scholarship has played a key role in providing content and justification of policies undertaken by international capital. Rereading has highlighted the continuing importance of the "directionality of the first-third world power relationship" (Mohanty 1991b: 72). Demonstrating the continuity between soft-state theory and World Bank policy points to the close relationship between theory and practice and the importance of deconstructing the way in which contemporary development theory colonizes the Third World through its binary logic that posits the modern (male) West as the norm and the traditional (female) Third World as the aberration. Dependency theory, in a different manner, has also produced a particular view of social structures in the Third World that creates a gendered analysis of the meaning of development and revolutionary politics. Rereading dependency theory demonstrates that a commitment to Third World resistance struggles against multinational capital, while extremely important, do not guarantee a nuanced analysis of gender and gender politics. Rereading these theories of development and underdevelopment demonstrates that approaches that either challenge or support the existing order are continuously altered and should still be read. For example, the shift in the representation of African women in late 1980s World Bank theory should be read alongside the Bank's focus on reducing women's fertility and its view of women as potential contributors to what Kardam (1991: 71) describes as the Bank's "neoliberal value system," one that stresses "capital accumulation and export expansion." The representation of women as the chief bearers of tradition in revolutionary discourse coincides with and reinforces Bank ideology, as governments such as Angola and Mozambique are subjected to the neoliberal discipline of structural adjustment. In both accounts, the "Third World woman" becomes the site where the goals of growth and capitalist expansion can be realized: Third World woman becomes a "safety net," and a "productive worker," while maintaining her role as chief nurturer within the nuclear family, and scapegoat for failed economic policy (Fatton 1989b).

Rereading also suggests the importance of understanding women as agents who "make choices, have a critical perspective on their own situations, and think and organize collectively against their oppressors" (Mohanty 1991a: 29). Rereading highlights the urgency of exploring the ways in which representations of women inform their subjectivity and the way women challenge efforts to construct the category of "woman."

Female-sphere advocates insist on the need to valorize women's experience as a means of challenging gender oppression. Embracing diversity and calling for the expression of each woman's authentic (and superior) experience is a position that valorizes "permissive heterogeneity" and a "rigid differentiation of outlooks between authenticated female viewpoints" (Goetz 1991: 146). One of the most promising alternatives to female-sphere cultural feminism are feminist standpoint theories (outlined in following pages).

Feminist standpoint theories attempt to go beyond the purported point-of-viewlessness of liberalism and the experience of the male proletariat in order to ground feminist theory in women's lives. Harding (1991: 106) describes feminist standpoint theory as an effort to give women a "voice of authority" and an opportunity for reconsidering what counts as knowledge. Hartsock (1983: 246) claims that the "articulation of a feminist standpoint based on women's relational self-definition and activity exposes the world men have constructed . . . as both partial and perverse." Jagger (1983: 371) emphasizes that a feminist standpoint is a political achievement. Taking a survey of women's attitudes toward particular issues is not the way to discern a standpoint; rather, a standpoint is a political accomplishment; an achievement. Harding (1991: 124) agrees that "mere" experiences and women's voices are necessary but not sufficient in the formulation of a standpoint: it is, rather, the "subsequently articulated observations of and theory about the rest of nature and social relations" that comprise a standpoint. Nevertheless, this approach risks ignoring the most important aspects of feminist theory's recent contribution to our understanding of the subject and the multiple and contradictory locations of "woman." In some ways it still asks to "include women" in development debates, thus legitimizing a term that should itself be posed as a theoretical problem. Theories of development and underdevelopment both should be read as narratives that rely heavily on gender as a means of making sense of modernity and tradition. The field of development studies is thus implicated in systematic practicies that ensure women's subordination. Challenges to development theory's totalizing and gendered logic about the meaning of both modernity and revolution, including WID theorizing and efforts to articulate difference, should acknowledge the extent to which these approaches continue to work within a theoretical frame of reference that promotes the achievement of "development" as it has been defined by modernization theory, dependency theory, and their more recent offshoots, soft-state theory and modes-of-production theory.

This study suggests that feminist standpoint theory can be valuable at two levels. First, rereading itself has provided a feminist standpoint on development theory. Questions have been raised about the construction of concepts, the binary logic of development theory, and the partial and distorted definition of development that results from the use of essentialized gender categories. Critical analysis and insistence about the need to reexamine fundamental renderings of tradition, modernity, and development have been a pervasive theme in this study.

At another level, feminist standpoint theory draws attention to the importance of studying acts of resistance and challenges to the practices of revolutionary states, capitalist states, and international donors. The strength of standpoint theory is its refusal to embrace an empiricist vision of experience "in which the individual subject's relationship to her world is taken to be direct and concrete, unmediated by the ways of making sense historically available to her" (Hennessy 1993a: 15). However, Hennessy also points to the gap between feminist discourse and "women's lives" (1993a: 15); the latter term is especially problematic because it assumes a coherent category of woman, ignores difference, and recreates the very practices that feminist theory seeks to subvert. Hennessy (1993a: 16) persuasively argues that feminist standpoint theory should be accompanied by a project that understands social relations in systemic terms, by which she means

> a perspective that addresses social systems—structures of power like capitalism, patriarchy, or colonialism—and posits connections between and among them. Marxism's usefulness for feminism is that it understands the social in precisely these terms—as an ensemble of economic, political, and ideological arrangements.

Such an approach avoids the postmodernist and deconstructive impulse that makes feminist theory impossible if not futile. As Goetz (1991: 148) remarks, "If gender or race or class are constructs with no essential core to liberate they are incapable of validating conceptions of justice or alternative truths." In other words, the insistence on the possibility of achieving a feminist standpoint must also recognize that such a standpoint is embedded in structures of power— what Di Stefano (1991b: 199) has called the "structured texture of politics." Such an approach could be a promising direction for development theory. While rereading suggests the urgency of dismantling gender dualisms and the binary logic of much of development theory, it seems counterproductive to stop there. Being sensitive to the systemic aspects of power and the systematic ways in which race, class, and gender structure people's lives has possibilities for rewriting the meaning of "development," which after all is not only a text but a continuing effort by people and movements to realize their aspirations (Lazarus 1990: 163).

This effort to rethink modernization and dependency theory suggests that attempts to theorize new meanings of development will be a formidable task. This is because development studies rest so firmly within a dualistic framework that constantly produces binary oppositions that limit both thought and practice. Within this framework, political strategies are posed in *either/or* terms—a logic that demands we choose one or the other side of the oppositions. Twenty years of WID and revolutionary politics in the Third World demonstrate that these categories need to be reconsidered and reconstituted. Upward mobility by joining the ranks of the moderns or maintaining reproductive and productive labor in the household for larger revolutionary purposes are indeed impoverished choices.

Postmodernist theorizing about the subject has eroded many of the many modernist claims that the modern state absorbs and dissolves all difference in the name of development and modernization. Rewriting development should begin with the household. It should critically question the treatment of the household in development studies. WID's "equal time" approach to the household—insisting that household labor is as productive as labor in a factory or on a state farm fails to theorize the historical development of different types of labor and the meanings attached to them. An alternative approach would have to locate the household in the worldwide system of capitalism, while recognizing and affirming the different labor women engage in. Such an approach might provide a vehicle through which we reconsider what it means to be modern, and suggest that a newly constituted theory of development could contribute to a critique of the modern embrace of industrialization and growth at all costs. In this sense, efforts to rewrite development could be viewed as attempts to transcend modernist discourse.

Efforts to rewrite development should also focus on the state and the way in which it complies with structural adjustment programs (SAPs) and facilitates capitalist restructuring. The state is an important force for implementing SAPs: it works to legitimate liberal definitions of democracy that ensure an order amenable to capitalism. Efforts to rewrite development can work to redefine the meaning of democracy—from one that rests on the stability and order of multiparty elections to a new and broader meaning that contests current liberal meanings of democracy. Reinterpreting democracy from the standpoint of women's lives in Africa and other areas of the Third World produces both a critical standpoint on existing practices and has the potential to provide a new set of alternatives to modernization, development, and revolution.

▲ Notes

1. Classic works on attempts to characterize the structure of the postcolonial state include Saul (1979), Shivji (1976), and Alavi (1982).

▲

References

Africa Contemporary Record. 1984–1985. Colin Legum, ed. *Annual Survey and Documents.* London: Rex Collings.

Ahmad, Aijaz. 1983. "Imperialism and Progress." In Ronald H. Chilcote and Dale L. Johnson, eds., *Theories of Development: Mode of Production or Dependency?* Beverly Hills: Sage.

Ake, Claude. 1985. "Introduction: The State in Contemporary Africa." In Ake, ed., *Political Economy of Nigeria.* New York: Longman.

———. 1985. "The Nigerian State: Antinomies of a Periphery Formation." In Ake, ed., *Political Economy of Nigeria.* New York: Longman.

Alavi, Hamza. 1982. "State and Class Under Peripheral Capitalism." In Hamza Alavi and Teodor Shanin, eds., *The Sociology of 'Developing Societies'.* New York: Monthly Review Press.

Almond, Gabriel. 1988. "The Return to the State." *American Political Science Review* 82: 853–874.

Amin, Samir. 1973. *Neo-Colonialism in West Africa.* New York: Monthly Review Press.

———. 1974a. "Accumulation and Development: A Theoretical Model." *Review of African Political Economy* 1: 9–26.

———. 1974b. *Accumulation on a World Scale.* 2 vols. New York: Monthly Review Press.

———. 1977. *Imperialism and Unequal Development.* New York: Monthly Review Press.

———. 1982. "The Disarticulation of Economy Within 'Developing Societies.'" In Hamza Alavi and Teodor Shanin, eds., *The Sociology of 'Developing Societies.'* New York: Monthly Review Press.

———. 1987. "Introduction." In Amin, Derrick Chitala, and Ibbo Mandaza, eds., *SADCC: Prospects for Disengagement and Development in Southern Africa.* London: Zed Press.

———. 1990. "Social Movements in the Periphery: An End to National Liberation?" In Amin, et al., *Transforming the Revolution: Social Movements in the Periphery.* New York: Monthly Review Press.

Anyaoku, Emeka. 1989. "Keynote Address: Impact of IMF–World Bank Policies on the People of Africa." In Bade Onimode, ed., *The IMF, the World Bank, and African Debt* Vol. 1. London: Zed Press.

Arnfred, Signe. 1988. "Women in Mozambique: Gender Struggle and Gender Politics." *Review of African Political Economy* 41: 5–16.

Avineri, Shlomo. 1968. *Karl Marx: Social and Political Thought.* London: Cambridge University Press.

135

Balbus, Isaac. 1982. *Marxism and Domination: A Neo-Hegelian, Feminist, Psycho-analytic Theory of Sexual, Political, and Technological Liberation.* Princeton: Princeton University Press.

Bandarage, Asoka. 1984. "Women in Development: Liberalism, Marxism, and Marxist-Feminism." *Development and Change* 15: 495–515.

Banuazizi, Ali. 1987. "Social-Psychological Approaches to Development." In Myron Weiner and Samuel P. Huntington, eds., *Understanding Political Development.* Boston: Little, Brown.

Bernstein, Henry. 1990. "Agricultural 'Modernization' and the Era of Structural Adjustment: Observations on Sub-Saharan Africa." *Journal of Peasant Studies* 18: 3–36.

Binder, Leonard. 1971. "Crises of Political Development." In Leonard Binder, et al., *Crises and Sequences in Political Development.* Princeton: Princeton University Press.

Bloch, Maurice, and Jean H. Bloch. 1980. "Women and the Dialectics of Nature in Eighteenth Century French Thought." in Carol P. MacCormack and Marilyn Strathern, eds., *Nature, Culture, and Gender.* Cambridge: Cambridge University Press.

Bluh, B. J. 1982. *Parson's General Theory of Social Action.* Granada Hills, California: NBS.

Boserup, Esther. 1970. *Women's Role in Economic Development.* London: George Allen and Unwin.

Bratton, Michael. 1989. "Beyond the State: Civil Society and Associational Life in Africa." *World Politics* 21: 407–430.

Bratton, Michael, and Donald Rothchild. 1992. "The Institutional Basis of Governing in Africa." in Goran Hyden and Michael Bratton, eds., *Governance and Politics in Africa.* Boulder: Lynne Rienner.

Brenner, Robert. 1977. "The Origins of Capitalist Development: A Critique of Neo-Smithian Marxism." *New Left Review* 104: 25–92.

Bridgland, Fred. 1986. *Jonas Savimbi: A Key to Africa.* New York: Paragon House.

Brown, Wendy. 1988. *Manhood and Politics: A Feminist Reading in Political Theory.* Totowa, New Jersey: Rowman and Littlefield.

———. 1992. "Finding the Man in the State." *Feminist Studies* 18: 7–35.

Callaghy, Thomas M. 1984. *The State-Society Struggle: Zaire in Comparative Perspective.* New York: Columbia University Press.

Cardoso, Fernando Henrique. 1977. "The Consumption of Dependency Theory in the United States." *Latin American Research Review* 12: 7–25.

———, and Enzo Faletto. 1979. *Dependency and Development in Latin America.* M. M. Urquiedi, trans. Berkeley: University of California Press.

Chan, Steve. 1987. "The Taiwan Exception: Implications for Contending Political Economy Paradigms." *International Studies Quarterly* 31: 327–356.

Charlton, Sue Ellen. 1989. *Women, the State, and Development.* Albany: State University of New York Press.

Charney, Craig. 1987. "Political Power and Social Class in the Neo-Colonial African State." *Review of African Political Economy* 38: 48–65.

Chazan, Naomi, et al. 1992. *Politics and Society in Contemporary Africa.* Boulder: Lynne Rienner.

Chodorow, Nancy. 1989. *Feminism and Psychoanalytic Theory.* New Haven, Connecticut: Yale University Press.

Clarence-Smith, Gervase. 1989. "The Roots of Mozambican Counterrevolution." *Southern Africa Review of Books* 2: 7–10.

Clark, Cal. 1987. "The Taiwan Exception: Implications for Contending Political Economy Paradigms." *International Studies Quarterly* 31: 327–358.

Cliffe, Lionel. 1982. "Class Formation as an 'Articulation' Process: East African Cases." In Hamza Alavi and Teodor Shanin, eds., *Introduction to the Sociology of 'Developing' Societies.* New York: Monthly Review Press.

————. 1987. "The Debate on African Peasantries." *Development and Change* 18: 625–635.

Coleman, James C. 1971. "The Development Syndrome: Differentiation-Equality-Capacity." In Leonard Binder, et al., *Crises and Sequences of Political Development.* Princeton: Princeton University Press.

Currie, Kate, and Larry Ray. 1984. "State and Class in Kenya: Notes on the Cohesion of the Ruling Class." *Journal of Modern African Studies* 22: 559–593.

Dash, Leon. 1977a. "Ambushing an Unwary Enemy." *Washington Post* August 7: A 24.

————. 1977b. "What Leads Guerrillas to Fight On?" *Washington Post* August 9: A8.

————. 1977c. "Politics Taught By Fable." *Washington Post* August 11: A8.

Davidson, Andrew. 1989. "Mode of Production: Impasse or Passe?" *Journal of Contemporary Asia* 19: 243–278.

De Groot, Joanna. 1991. "Conceptions and Misconceptions: The Historical and Cultural Context of Discussion of Women and Development." In Haleh Afshar, ed., *Women, Development, and Survival in the Third World.* London: Longman.

Devereux, Edward C., Jr. 1961. "Parson's Sociological Theory." In Max E. Black, ed., *The Social Theories of Talcott Parsons.* Englewood Cliffs, New Jersey: Prentice-Hall.

Di Stefano, Christine. 1991a. *Configurations of Masculinity: A Feminist Perspective on Modern Political Theory.* Ithaca, New York: Cornell University Press.

————. 1991b. "Masculine Marx." In Mary Lyndon Shanley and Carole Pateman, eds., *Feminist Interpretations and Political Theory.* University Park, Pennsylvania: Pennsylvania State University Press.

Doornbos, Martin. 1990. "The African State in Academic Debate: Retrospect and Prospect." *The Journal of Modern African Studies*: 179–198.

Edwards, Michael. 1989. "The Irrelevance of Development Studies." *Third World Quarterly* 11: 116–135.

Ekeh, Peter. 1975. "Colonialism and the Two Publics in Africa: A Theoretical Statement." *Comparative Studies in Society and History* 17: 91–112.

Elshtain, Jean Bethke. 1981. *Public Man, Private Woman.* New Haven, Connecticut: Yale University Press.

Elson, Diane. 1989. "The Impact of Structural Adjustment on Women." In Bade Onimode, ed., *The IMF, the World Bank, and African Debt* vol. 2. London: Zed Press.

————. 1992. "From Survival Strategies to Transformation Strategies: Women's Needs and Structural Adjustment." in Lourdes Beneria and Shelley Feldman, eds., *Unequal Burden: Economic Crisis, Persistent Povery, and Women's Work.* Boulder: Westview Press.

Fatton, Robert. 1988. "Bringing the Ruling Classes Back In: Class, State, and Hegemony in Africa." *Comparative Politics* 20: 253–264.

————. 1989a. "The State of African Studies and Studies of the African State: The Theoretical Softness of the 'Soft State.'" *Journal of Asian and African Studies* 24: 170–188.

138   *Gender and Development*

———. 1989b. "Gender, Class, and State in Africa." In Jane Parpart and Kathleen Staudt, eds., *Women and the State in Africa*. Boulder: Lynne Rienner.

Ferguson, Kathy E. 1990. "Women, Feminism, and Development." in Kathleen Staudt, ed., *Women, International Politics, and Development: The Bureaucratic Mire*. Philadelphia: Temple University Press.

Finkel, Vicki R. 1992. "Brothers in Arms." *Africa Report* 37: 63–64.

Flax, Jane. 1983. "Political Philosophy and the Patriarchal Unconscious: A Psychoanalytic Perspective on Epistemology and Metaphysics." In Sandra Harding and Merrill Hintikka, eds., *Discovering Reality: Perspectives on Epistemology, Metaphysics, and Philosophy of Science*. Dordrecht, Holland: D. Reidel.

Forrest, Joshua. 1988. "The Quest for State 'Hardness' in Africa." *Comparative Politics* 20: 423–443.

Foster-Carter, Aidan. 1978. "The Modes of Production Controversy." *New Left Review* 107: 47–77.

Frank, Andre Gundar. 1966. "The Development of Underdevelopment." *Monthly Review* 18: 17–31.

———. 1969a. *Latin America: Underdevelopment or Revolution. Essays on the Development of Underdevelopment and the Immediate Enemy*. New York: Monthly Review Press.

———. 1969b. *Capitalism and Underdevelopment in Latin America: Historical Studies of Chile and Brazil* revised. New York: Monthly Review Press.

———. 1972. "The Development of Underdevelopment." In James D. Cockcroft, Andre Gundar Frank, and Dale L. Johnson, eds., *Dependence and Underdevelopment: Latin America's Political Economy*. New York: Monthly Review Press.

———. 1979. *Dependent Accumulation and Underdevelopment*. New York: Monthly Review Press.

Frelimo—Frente de Libertaçao de Mocambique. 1983. *Out of Underdevelopment to Socialism*. Maputo.

Gallin, Rita S., and Anne Ferguson. 1991. *The Women and International Development Annual* vol. 2. Boulder: Westview Press.

Gendzier, Irene. 1985. *Managing Political Change: Social Scientists and the Third World*. Boulder: Westview Press.

Gibbon, Peter, and Michael Neocosmos. 1985. "Some Problems in the Political Economy of 'African Socialism.'" In Henry Bernstein and Bonnie K. Campbell, eds., *Contradictions of Accumulation in Africa*. Beverly Hills: Sage.

Gladwin, Christina, ed. 1991. *Structural Adjustment and African Women Farmers*. Gainesville: University of Florida Press.

Goetz, Ann Marie. 1991. "Feminism and the Claim to Know: Contradictions in Feminist Approaches to Women and Development." In Rebecca Grant and Kathleen Newland, eds., *Gender and International Relations*. Bloomington: Indiana University Press.

Grant, Judith. 1987. "I Feel Therefore I Am: A Critique of Female Experience as a Basis for Feminist Epistemology." *Women and Politics* 7: 99–114.

Gregory, Donna. 1989. "Foreword." In James Der Derian and Michael J. Shapiro, eds. *International/Intertextual Relations*. Lexington, Massachusetts: Lexington Books.

Gross, Michael, and Mary Beth Averill. 1983. "Evolution and Patriarchal Myths of Scarcity and Competition." In Sandra Harding and Merrill B. Hintikka, eds., *Discovering Reality: Feminist Perspectives on Epistemology,*

Metaphysics, Methodology, and Philosophy of Science. Dordrect, Holland: D. Reidel.
Hall, Margaret. 1990. "The Mozambique National Resistance and South African Foreign Policy." *Africa* (London) 60: 39–68.
Hanlon, Joseph. 1984. *Mozambique: The Revolution Under Fire.* London: Zed Press.
Haraway, Donna. 1978. "Animal Sociology and a Natural Economy of the Body Politic, Part 1: A Political Physiology of Dominance." *Signs* 4: 21–36.
Harding, Sandra. 1991. *Whose Science? Whose Knowledge? Thinking From Women's Lives.* Ithaca: Cornell University Press.
Harris, Laurence. 1989. "The Bretton Woods System and Africa." In Bade Onimode, ed., *The IMF, the World Bank, and African Debt* vol. 1. London: Zed Press.
Harsch, Ernest, with Roy Laishley. 1993. "Mozambique: Out of the Ruins of War." *Africa Recovery* briefing paper 8 (May).
Hartsock, Nancy. 1983. *Money, Sex, and Power: Toward a Feminist Historical Materialism.* New York: Longman.
Harwood, Richard. 1981a. "Rebel Goal: An End to Foreign Control." *Washington Post* July 20: A8.
———. 1981b. "Guerrillas Demonstrate High Morale." *Washington Post* July 22: A15.
Heilbroner, Robert. 1980. *Marx: For and Against.* New York: W. W. Norton.
Hennessy, Rosemary. 1993a. "Women's Lives/Feminist Knowledge: Feminist Standpoint as Ideology Critique." *Hypatia* 8: 14–34.
———. 1993b. *Materialist Feminism and the Politics of Discourse.* New York: Routledge.
Heywood, Linda. 1987. "The Growth and Decline of African Agriculture in Central Angola." *Journal of Southern African Studies* 13: 355–371.
———. 1989. "UNITA and Ethnic Nationalism in Angola." *Journal of Modern African Studies* 27: 47–66.
Hirschmann, Nancy. 1989. "Freedom, Recognition, and Obligation: A Feminist Approach to Political Theory." *American Political Science Review* 83: 122–1245.
Holt, Robert T., and John E. Turner. 1975. "Crises and Sequences in Collective Theory Development." *American Political Science Review* 69: 979–994.
Huntington, Samuel P. 1968. *Political Order in Changing Societies.* New Haven: Yale University Press.
———. 1987. "The Goals of Political Development." In Myron P. Weiner and Samuel P. Huntington, eds., *Understanding Political Development.* Boston: Little, Brown.
Hyden, Goran. 1980. *Beyond Ujamaa in Tanzania: Underdevelopment and an Uncaptured Peasantry.* Berkeley: University of California Press.
———. 1983a. *No Shortcuts to Progress: African Development Management in Perspective.* Berkeley: University of California Press.
———. 1983b. "Problems and Prospects of State Coherence." In Donald Rothchild and Victor Olorunsula, eds., *State vs. Ethnic Claims: African Policy Dilemmas.* Boulder: Westview Press.
———. 1985. "Urban Growth and Rural Development." In Gwendolyn M. Carter and Patrick O'Meara, eds., *African Independence: The First Twenty-Five Years.* Bloomington: Indiana University Press.
———. 1986. "African Social Structure and Economic Development." In Robert J. Berg and Jennifer Seymour Whittaker, eds., *Strategies for African Development.* Berkeley: University of California Press.

————. 1987. "Capital Accumulation, Resource Distribution, and Governance in Kenya: The Role of the Economy of Affection." In Michael G. Schatzberg, ed., *The Political Economy of Kenya.* New York: Praeger.

————. 1989. "Governance and Liberalization: Tanzania in Comparative Perspective." Paper presented at the American Political Science Association annual meeting.

————. 1990. "Reciprocity and Governance in Africa." In James D. Wunsch and Dele Olowu, eds., *The Failure of the Centralized State: Institutions and Self-Governance in Africa.* Boulder: Westview Press.

————. 1992. "Governance and the Study of Politics." In Hyden and Michael Bratton, eds., *Governance and Politics in Africa.* Boulder: Lynne Rienner.

————, and Pauline Peters. 1991. "Debate on the Economy of Affection: Is it a Useful Tool for Gender Analysis?" In Christina Gladwin, ed., *Structural Adjustment and African Women Farmers.* Gainesville, Florida: University of Florida Press.

Inkeles, Alex. 1969. "Participant Citizenship in Six Developing Countries." *American Political Science Review* 63: 1120–1141.

————, and David H. Smith. 1974. *Becoming Modern: Individual Change in Six Developing Countries.* Cambridge: Harvard University Press.

————, David H. Smith, et al. 1983. *Exploring Individual Modernity.* New York: Columbia University Press.

Isaacman, Barbara, and June Stephen. 1980. *Mozambique: Women, the Law, and Agrarian Reform.* Addis Ababa: U.N. Economic Commission for Africa.

Jackson, Robert H. and Carl G. Rosberg. 1982. *Personal Rule in Black Africa: Prince, Autocrat, Prophet, Tyrant.* Berkeley: University of California Press.

Jagger, Alison. 1983. *Feminist Politics and Human Nature.* Totowa, New Jersey: Rowman and Littlefield.

Jaquette, Jane. 1982. "Women and Modernization Theory: A Decade of Criticism." *World Politics* 39: 267–289.

Johnson, Dale. 1972. "Dependence and the International System." In James D. Cockcroft, Andre Gundar Frank, and Dale L. Johnson, eds., *Dependence and Underdevelopment: Latin America's Political Economy.* New York: Anchor: 71–115.

Johnston, Deborah. 1991. "Constructing the Periphery in Modern Global Politics." in Craig N. Murphy and Roger Tooze, eds., *The International Political Economy.* Boulder: Lynne Rienner.

Jones, Kathleen., 1990. "Citizenship in a Woman-Friendly Polity." *Signs* 15: 781–812.

Jordanova, L. J. 1980. "Natural Facts: A Historical Perspective on Science and Sexuality." In Carol P. MacCormack and Marilyn Strathern, eds., *Nature, Culture, and Gender.* London: Cambridge University Press.

Kardam, Nuket. 1990. "The Adaptability of International Development Agencies: The Response of the World Bank to Women in Development." in Kathleen Staudt, ed., *Women in Development.*

————. 1991. *Bringing Women In: Women's Issues in International Development Programs.* Boulder: Lynne Rienner.

Kasfir, Nelson. 1986. "Are African Peasants Self-Sufficient?" *Development and Change* 17: 335–357.

Keller, Evelyn Fox. 1990. "Gender and Science." In Joyce McCarl Nielson, ed., *Feminist Research Methods: Exemplary Readings in the Social Sciences.* Boulder: Westview Press.

Kruks, Sonia, and Ben Wisner. 1984. "The State, the Party, and the Female Peasantry in Mozambique." *Journal of Southern African Studies* 11: 106–128.

Kruks, Sonia, and Ben Wisner. 1989. "Ambiguous Transformations: Women, Politics, and Production in Mozambique." in Kruks, Rayna Rapp, and Marilyn B. Young, eds. 1989. *Promissory Notes: Women and the Transition to Socialism.* New York: Monthly Review Press: 148–171.

LaPalombara, Joseph. 1971. "Penetration: A Crisis of Governmental Capacity." In Leonard Binder, et al., *Crises and Sequences of Political Development.* Princeton: Princeton University Press.

Lazarus, Neil. 1990. "Imperialism, Cultural Theory, and Radical Intellectualism Today: A Critical Assessment." *Rethinking Marxism* 3: 156–165.

Lemarchand, Rene. 1989. "African Peasantries, Reciprocity, and the Market." *Cahiers d'Etudes Africaines* 113: 33–67.

Lerner, Daniel. 1958. *The Passing of Traditional Society: Modernizing the Middle East.* New York: Free Press.

Lloyd, Genevieve. 1984. *The Man of Reason: "Male" and "Female" in Western Philosophy.* Minneapolis: University of Minnesota Press.

Loxley, John. 1991. "Structural Adjustment in Africa: Reflections on Ghana and Zambia." *Review of African Political Economy* 47: 8–28.

Lukes, Steven. 1978. *Individualism.* London: Blackwell Publishers.

Machel, Samora. 1981. *Mozambique: Sowing the Seeds of Revolution.* Harare, Zimbabwe: Zimbabwe Publishing House.

Mackintosh, Maureen. 1990. "Abstract Markets and Real Needs." In Henry Bernstein, et al., eds., *The Food Question: People vs. Profits.* London: Earthscan.

Macpherson, C. B. 1962. *The Political Theory of Possessive Individualism.* London: Oxford University Press.

———. 1973. *Democratic Theory: Essays in Retrieval.* Oxford: Clarendon Press.

Mamdani, Mahmood. 1985. "A Great Leap Backward: A Review of Goran Hyden's *No Shortcuts to Progress.*" *Ufamahu* 14: 178–195.

Marshall, Judith. 1990. "Structural Adjustment and Social Policy in Mozambique." *Review of African Political Economy* 47: 28–44.

Marx, Karl. (1978). "Capital, Volume One" (selections). In Robert Tucker, ed., *The Marx-Engels Reader* 2d ed. New York: W. W. Norton.

McClelland, David C. 1976. *The Achieving Society* reprint. New York: Irvington.

McMurtry, John. 1978. *The Structure of Marx's Worldview.* Princeton: Princeton University Press.

Mbilinyi, Marjorie. 1990. "Structural Adjustment, Agribusiness, and Rural Women in Tanzania." In Henry Bernstein, et al., eds., *The Food Question: Profits vs. People.* London: Earthscan.

Medley, Joseph. 1989. "Concepts of Capital Accumulation and Economic Development: Samir Amin's Contradictions." *Rethinking Marxism* 2: 83–104.

Melotti, Umberto. 1977. *Marx and the Third World.* Pat Ransford, trans. London: Macmillan.

Mills, Patricia Jagentowicz. 1991. "Feminism and Ecology: On the Domination of Nature." *Hypatia* 6: 162–178.

Mitchell, Timothy. 1991. "The Limits of the State: Beyond Statist Approaches and Their Critics." *American Political Science Review* 85: 77–98.

Mittelman, James. 1991. "Marginalization and the International Division of Labor: Mozambique's Strategy of Opening the Market." *African Studies Review* 34: 89–106.

Mkandawire, P. Thankdika. 1983. "Accumulation on a World Scale." In Peter Limqueco and Bruce McFarlane, eds., *Neo-Marxist Theories of Development*. London: Croom Helm: 50–58.

Mohanty, Chandra Talpade. 1991a. "Cartographies of Struggle: Third World Women and the Politics of Feminism." In Mohanty, Ann Russo, and Lourdes Torres, eds., *Third World Women and the Politics of Feminism*. Bloomington: University of Indiana Press.

———. 1991b. "Under Western Eyes: Feminist Scholarship and Colonial Discourses." In Mohanty, Ann Russo, and Lourdes Torres, eds., *Third World Women and the Politics of Feminism*. Bloomington, Indiana: Indiana University Press.

Molyneux, Maxine. 1986. "Mobilization without Emancipation? Women's Interests, the State, and Revolution." In Richard R. Fagen, Carmen Diana Deere, and Jose Luis Coraggio, eds., *Transition and Development: Problems of Third World Socialism*. New York: Monthly Review Press: 280–302.

———. 1991. "Marxism, Feminism, and the Demise of the Soviet Model." In Rebecca Grant and Kathleen Newland, eds., *Gender and International Relations*. Bloomington: Indiana University Press.

Moore, Barrington. 1966. *The Social Origins of Dictatorship and Democracy*. Boston: Beacon Press.

Morgan, Glenda. 1990. "Violence in Mozambique: Toward an Understanding of Renamo." *Journal of Modern African Studies* 28: 603–619.

MPLA—Movimento Popular de Libertacao de Angola. 1977. *First Congress of the MPLA: Report to the Central Committee*. Luanda, Angola.

Munslow, Barry. 1984. "Intervention in Agriculture: The Mozambique Experience." *Journal of Modern African Studies* 22: 199–223.

———. 1985. *Samora Machel: An African Revolutionary: Selected Speeches and Writings*. Michael Wolfers, trans. London: Zed Press.

Myrdal, Gunnar. 1968. *Asian Drama* 3 vols. New York: Twentieth Century Fund.

Nandy, Ashis. 1983. *The Intimate Enemy: Loss and Recovery of Self under Colonialism*. London and New Delhi: Oxford University Press.

Nicholson, Linda. 1987. "Feminism and Marx: Integrating the Kinship with the Economic." In Seyla Benhabib and Drucilla Cornell, eds., *Feminism as Critique: On the Politics of Gender*. Minneapolis: University of Minnesota Press.

Nyang'oro, Julius. 1989. *The State and Capitalist Development in Africa: Declining Political Economies*. New York: Praeger.

O'Brien, Mary. 1981. *The Politics of Reproduction*. London: Routledge and Kegan Paul.

Okin, Susan Moller. 1979. *Women in Western Political Thought*. Princeton: Princeton: University Press.

Ollman, Bertel. 1971. *Alienation: Marx's Conception of Man in Capitalist Society*. London: Cambridge University Press.

Ong, Bie Nie. 1986. "Women and the Transition to Socialism in Subsaharan Africa." In Barry Munslow, ed., *Africa: Problems in the Transition to Socialism*. London: Zed Press.

Onimode, Badi, ed. 1989. *The IMF, the World Bank, and the African Debt*. Volume One: The Economic Impact. London: Zed Press.

OMA—Organizacao das Mulheres de Angola. 1984 *Angolan Women Building the Future*. Margaret Holness, trans. London: Zed Press.

Ortner, Sherry. 1974. "Is Female to Male as Nature Is to Culture?" In Michelle Zimbalist Rosaldo, ed., *Woman, Culture, and Society*. Stanford, California: Stanford University Press.

Ottaway, David, and Marina Ottaway. 1986. *Afrocommunism.* Second edition. New York: Holmes and Meier.

Ottaway, Marina. 1988. "Mozambique: From Symbolic Socialism to Symbolic Reform." *Journal of Modern African Studies* 26: 211–226.

Paarlberg, Robert, and Michael Lipton. 1991. "Changing Missions at the World Bank." *World Policy Journal* 8: 475–499.

Packenham, Robert A. 1973. *Liberal America and the Third World.* Princeton: Princeton University Press.

Parsons, Talcott. 1960. *Structure and Process in Modern Societies.* New York: Free Press.

———. 1964. "Evolutionary Universals in Society." *American Journal of Sociology* 29: 339–358.

Pazzanita, Anthony. 1991. "The Conflict Resolution Process in Angola." *Journal of Modern African Studies* 29: 83–114.

Peterson, V. Spike. 1992. "Transgressing Boundaries: Theories of Knowledge, Gender, and International Relations." *Millenium* 21: 183–209.

Portes, Alejandro. 1976. "On the Sociology of National Development: Theories and Issues." *American Journal of Sociology* 82: 55–85.

Pye, Lucian. 1971a. "Foreword." In Leonard Binder, et al., *Crises and Sequences of Political Development.* Princeton: Princeton University Press.

———. 1971b. "Identity and the Political Culture." In Leonard Binder, et al., *Crises and Sequences of Political Development.* Princeton: Princeton University Press.

Randall, Vicky, and Robin Theobald. 1985. *Political Change and Underdevelopment: A Critical Introduction to Third World Politics.* Durham, North Carolina: Duke University Press.

Rey, Phillippe. 1973. *Les Alliances de Classes.* Maspero: Paris.

Rodney, Walter, 1981. *How Europe Underdeveloped Africa* revised. Washington, D.C.: Howard University Press.

Rooney, Phyllis. 1991. "Gendered Reason: Sex Metaphors and Conceptions of Reason." *Hypatia* 6: 77–104.

Rosberg, Carl G., and Thomas M. Callaghy, eds. 1979. *Socialism in Sub-Saharan Africa: A New Assessment.* Berkeley: University of California Press.

Rosenau, Pauline. 1992. *Post-Modernism and the Social Sciences: Insights, Inroads, and Intrusions.* Princeton: Princeton University Press.

Rostow, W. W. 1960. *The Stages of Economic Growth: A Non-Communist Manifesto.* Cambridge, England: Cambridge University Press.

Rothchild, Donald. 1985. "Hegemony and State Softness: Some Variations in Elite Responses." Paper presented at the African Studies Association, New Orleans, Louisiana (November).

———, and Naomi Chazan, eds. 1988. *The Precarious Balance: State and Society in Africa.* Boulder: Westview Press.

———, and Victor A. Olorunsola, eds. 1983. *State Versus Ethnic Claims: African Policy Dilemmas.* Boulder: Westview Press.

Ruccio, David, and Lawrence H. Simon. 1989. "Radical Theories of Development: Frank, the Modes of Production School, and Amin." In Charles K. Wilber, ed., *The Political Economy of Development and Underdevelopment* 4th ed. New York: Random House.

Rudolph, Lloyd I., and Susan Hoeber Rudolph. 1967. *The Modernity of Tradition: Political Development in India.* Chicago: University of Chicago Press.

SADCC—Southern African Development Coordination Conference. 1986. "Sub-regional Conference on Policy Implications on Women in Agricultural

Development for SADCC Member States." Lusaka, Zambia. October 6–10.

———. 1987. "Report on High Level Workshop to Formulate Strategies on the Integration of Women's Issues in SADCC Development Programs." Lusaka, Zambia (30 Nov.–4 Dec.).

———. 1988. "Women and Food Technologies in the SADCC Region vol. 1. Report on the SADCC Conference on Women and Food Technologies. Arusha, Tanzania (23–27 May).

———. 1991. "Human Resources: The Primary Factor in Development. Proceedings of the annual consultative conference. Windhoek, Namibia (31 Jan.–2 Feb.).

Said, Edward. 1979. *Orientalism.* New York: Vintage.

Samatar, Abdi, and A. I. Samatar. 1987. "The Material Roots of the Suspended African State: Arguments from Somalia." *Journal of Modern African Studies* 25: 669–690.

Sangmpam, S. N. 1993. "Neither Soft nor Dead: The African State Is Alive and Well." *African Studies Review* 36: 73–94.

Saul, John. 1979. "The State in Postcolonial Societies: Tanzania." In his *The State and Revolution in East Africa.* New York: Monthly Review Press.

Sawyerr, Akilagpa. 1990. "The Politics of Adjustment Policy." In Adebayo Adedeji, Sadiq Rasheed, and Melody Morrison, eds., *The Human Dimension of Africa's Persistent Economic Crisis.* London: Hans Zell.

Scott, Catherine V. 1986. *Political Development in Afromarxist Regimes: An Analysis of Angola and Mozambique.* Ph.D. dissertation, Emory University, Atlanta, Georgia.

———. 1988. "Socialism and the 'Soft State' in Africa: An Analysis of Angola and Mozambique." *Journal of Modern African Studies* 26: 23–36.

Seidman, Ann. 1989. "Towards Ending I.M.F.–ism in Southern Africa: An Alternative Development Strategy." *Journal of Modern African Studies* 27: 1–22.

Sen, Gita, and Caren Grown. 1987. *Development, Crises, and Alternative Visions: Third World Women's Perspectives.* New York: Monthly Review Press.

Shapiro, Jeremy. 1976. "The Slime of History: Embeddedness in Nature and Critical Theory." in John O'Neill, ed., *On Critical Theory.* New York: Seabury Press.

Shaw, Timothy. 1991. "Reformism, Revisionism, and Radicalism in African Political Economy During the 1990s." *Journal of Modern African Studies* 29: 191–212.

Shiva, Vandana. 1988. *Staying Alive: Women, Ecology, and Development.* London: Zed Press.

———. 1990. "Development as a New Project of Western Patriarchy." In Irene Diamond and Gloria Feman Orenstein, eds., *Reweaving the World: The Emergence of Ecofeminism.* San Francisco: Sierra Club Books.

Shivji, Issa. 1976. *Class Struggles in Tanzania.* New York: Monthly Review Press.

Skoçpol, Theda. 1985. "Bringing the State Back In: Strategies of Analysis in Current Research." In Peter B. Evans, Dietrich Rueschemeyer, and Theda Skoçpol, eds., *Bringing the State Back In.* Cambridge, England: Cambridge University Press.

Smith, Tony. 1985. "Requiem or New Agenda for Third World Studies?" *World Politics* 37: 532–561.

Thompson, Janna. 1986. "Women and Political Rationality." In Carole Pateman and Elizabeth Gross, eds., *Feminist Challenges: Social and Political Theory.* Boston: Northeastern University Press.

Tinker, Irene. 1990. "The Making of a Field: Advocates, Practitioners, and Scholars." In Tinker, ed., *Persistent Inequalities: Women and World Development.* New York: Oxford University Press.

Tipps, Dean. 1976. "Modernization Theory and the Comparative Study of Societies." In Cyril E. Black, ed., *Comparative Modernization.* New York: Free Press.

Tripp, Aili Mari. 1992. "The Impact of Crisis and Economic Reform on Women in Urban Tanzania." In Lourdes Beneria and Shelley Feldman, eds., *Unequal Burden: Economic Crises Persistent Poverty, and Women's Work.* Boulder: Westview Press.

Tucker, Robert, ed. 1978. *The Marx-Engels Reader* 2d ed. New York: W. W. Norton.

UNECA—United Nations Economic Commission for Africa. 1989. *African Alternative Framework to Structural Adjustment. Programs for Socio-Economic Recovery and Transformation.* Addis Ababa.

Urdang, Stephanie. 1983. "The Last Transition? Women and Development in Mozambique." *Review of African Political Economy* 27/28: 9–29.

———. 1985. "The Last Transition? Women and Development." In John Saul, ed. *The Difficult Road: The Transition to Socialism in Mozambique.* New York: Monthly Review Press.

———. 1989. *And Still They Dance: Women, War, and the Struggle for Change in Mozambique.* New York: Monthly Review Press.

Vandergeest, Peter, and Frederick Buttel. 1988. "Marx, Weber, and Development Sociology: Beyond the Impasse." *World Development* 16: 683–695.

Verba, Sidney. 1971. "Sequences and Development." in Binder, et al., *Crises and Sequences of Political Development.* Princeton: Princeton University Press: 283–316.

Vilas, Carlos. 1988. "War and Revolution in Nicaragua." In Ralph Miliband, Leo Panitch, and John Saville, eds., *Socialist Register, 1988.* London: Merlin Press.

Waters, Tony. 1992. "A Cultural Analysis of the Economy of Affection and the Uncaptured Peasantry in Tanzania." *Journal of Modern African Studies* 30: 163–175.

White, Frances E. 1990. "Africa on My Mind: Gender, Counter-Discourse, and African-American Nationalism." *Journal of Women's History* 2: 73–97.

Whitehead, Ann. 1990. "Food Crisis and Gender Conflict in the African Countryside." In Henry Bernstein, Ben Crow, Maureen MacIntosh, and Charlotte Martin, eds., *The Food Question: Profits vs. People.* New York: Monthly Review Press: 54–68.

Wolfers, Michael, and Jane Bergerol. 1983. *Angola in the Frontline.* London: Zed Press.

Wolin, Sheldon. 1960. *Politics and Vision: Continuity and Innovation in Western Political Thought.* Boston: Little, Brown.

World Bank. 1981. *Accelerated Development in Sub-Saharan Africa: An Agenda for Action.* Washington, D.C.: World Bank.

———. 1989. *Sub-Saharan Africa: From Crisis to Sustainable Growth. A Long-Term Perspective Study.* Washington, D.C.: World Bank.

Wunsh, James, and Dele Olowu, eds. 1990. *The Failure of the Centralized State: Institutions and Self-Governance in Africa.* Boulder: Westview Press.

Young, Crawford. 1984. *Ideology and Development in Africa.* New Haven: Yale University Press.

Young, Tom. 1989. "The MNR/Renamo: External and Internal Dynamics." *African Affairs:* 491–509.

▲
Index

▲

About the Book and the Author

Catherine V. Scott demonstrates that many prevailing ideas about development, dependency, capitalism, and socialism are anchored in social constructions of gender differences.

Early modernization theorists, points out Scott, often juxtaposed modernity and tradition in ways reminiscent of Enlightenment dichotomies that pitted the rational, productive city against the particularistic, fragmented, and stagnant countryside. Dependency theory, despite its radically difference focus on the causes of underdevelopment, also rests upon masculinist conceptions of the unfolding of history, human labor, and the gendered divisions between the public and private realms. Recent theories of the African "soft state," realized in policymaking, revive modernization theory's dichotomies; and revolutionary political leaders in African countries, though they have challenged imperialism, have retained the Marxist blind-spot regarding gender.

This provocative critique of both theory and practice goes beyond the "women in development" approach to explore fundamental reconceptualizations of tradition, modernity, masculinity, femininity, revolution, and development.

Catherine V. Scott is associate professor of political science at Agnes Scott College.